Resiliency

WHAT WE HAVE LEARNED

WestEd⊕   BONNIE BENARD

Printed in the United States of America.

ISBN: 978-0-914409-18-2
Library of Congress Control Number: 2003111887

WestEd, a national nonpartisan, nonprofit research, development, and service agency, works with education and other communities to promote excellence, achieve equity, and improve learning for children, youth, and adults. WestEd has 16 offices nationwide, from Washington and Boston to Arizona and California. Its corporate headquarters are in San Francisco.

WestEd books and products are available through bookstores and online booksellers. WestEd also publishes its books in a variety of electronic formats. To contact WestEd directly, call our Publications Center at 888-293-7833.

For more information about WestEd:

Visit www.WestEd.org

Call 415-565-3000 or toll free 877-4-WestEd

Write WestEd at 730 Harrison Street, San Francisco, CA 94107-1242

Contents

"What began as a quest to understand

the extraordinary has revealed the power

of the ordinary. Resilience does not come

from rare and special qualities, but from

the everyday magic of ordinary, normative

human resources in the minds, brains, and

bodies of children, in their families and

relationships, and in their communities."

— Ann Masten

Foreword

All of us have met individuals who overcame staggering challenges growing up. As their stories unfold before us, it is difficult not to wonder how they managed to become such positive and productive adults. So much of what we are asked to believe about young people facing similar challenges would have predicted their failure. But that is what Bonnie Benard's new book and, indeed, her whole career are about — letting the rest of us know that we human beings are all remarkable, that we have the capacity to thrive, and that we can all use a little help.

Bonnie Benard lives and breathes the belief that all people, particularly all children and youth, have enormous strengths. She also embodies the belief that as adults we are charged with helping young people build upon those assets, and so support them in becoming the adults they aspire to be, regardless of the conditions and challenges they encounter.

In *Resiliency: What We Have Learned*, Bonnie captures what she has learned throughout a career dedicated to seeking the positive, even when cultural forces and intellectual models have pointed others in her field to a more negative approach. She speaks of assets; others may identify deficits. She affirms and builds; many of us criticize and inadvertently tear down. I recently heard her tell the story of an after-school high school program that she considered excellent, yet to participate students were required to pass into a classroom labeled "At-Risk Youth," proclaiming an expectation not of success but of failure.

Bonnie's book sensitizes us to the implications of building up rather than tearing down. Like labels with their unintended messages, Bonnie asks us to look carefully at our approach to testing in this country — and whether our rhetoric that no child be left behind might be at odds with testing and retesting our children with a focus on what each child lacks. The unintended consequences for hundreds of thousands of students could be an experience of themselves as endlessly deficient rather than full of potential.

In synthesizing the resilience research of the last decade and more, and in analyzing key approaches for supporting young people, Bonnie illuminates a vision that I hope will be carefully explored by all educators and human service providers. It is also one for all parents to consider. The daily stresses and strains for children and youth are enormous, even for those who live in what appear to be the most positive of conditions. For me as a parent, Bonnie's work and coaching have been a mainstay as I seek to put aside the deficit model I internalized early on and instead find ways to support the unique strengths and magic that my two children possess. In reading this book, I have found renewed optimism and hope, together with concrete ways that I and others can make a difference for children and youth, our own and those whom our policies, practices, and initiatives can affect.

There is always a danger in highlighting research about how children in enormously challenging conditions may nevertheless survive and even thrive. Inevitably, some policymakers and practitioners interpret such findings as evidence that interventions, resources, and support are not necessary. That is not the message of *Resiliency: What We Have Learned*. This is not a "pull yourself up by the bootstraps" model. To the contrary. We all have roles to play and the responsibility to play them. Children are born with remarkable and unique gifts, qualities, and potential. As adults we need to rededicate ourselves to cherishing, nurturing, and supporting each child we can. The opportunity exists to make a difference in a child's life every time we make that small effort.

Glen Harvey
Chief Executive Officer
WestEd

A Pivotal Decade

It was over a decade ago when I first pulled together a summary of resilience research. The slim volume that resulted, *Fostering Resiliency in Kids,* has now grown to this less-slim volume, *Resiliency: What We Have Learned,* to reflect the fervor of interest, research, and programs about resilience — how children and youth overcome the odds to become "competent, confident, and caring" individuals (Werner & Smith, 1992) — that the last dozen years have brought. A simple but graphic measure of this attention is provided by the *Social Sciences Citation Index.* In the 1980s, "resilience" and its derivatives occurred only 24 times. In the 1990s, there were 735 such references. The current decade is on a pace to at least double the previous total output of scholarly research on the topic.

The recent past has been pivotal for all strengths-based movements — in education, prevention, and other human services. We now have considerable research and practitioner interest in resilience, youth development, asset-building, positive psychology, wellness, health promotion, health realization, strengths-based social work, social capital and its sub-categories, multiple intelligences, values-centered or spiritual intelligence, and emotional intelligence. Obviously, people in professions known for studying and ameliorating human problems are increasingly attracted to what has become a new paradigm, a new way of thinking about and working with human beings across the lifespan, but especially during the years of childhood and adolescence.

Unfortunately, even armed with new understandings and programs, practitioners face almost the same percentage of children and families living in extreme adversity as ten years ago. According to the latest Kids Count report from the Annie E. Casey Foundation (March 2002), the percentage of children living in "high-risk" families has dropped only 1 percent from 1990 to 2000. Twelve percent of American children continue to live not only below the poverty line, but in conditions not likely to improve — for example with parents who lack a high school diploma or full-time employment (2002, http://www.kidscount.org).

Similarly, the life conditions of non-college-bound youth and young families have barely improved in the last decade. In 1988, Samuel Halperin's two reports about this group, which he called "the forgotten half," stirred the education world with statistics about the grim outlook for this large segment of the American population. Ten years later, in *The Forgotten Half Revisited* (1998), Halperin is unable to report much improvement, and in some areas, such as employment and incarceration, must report alarming regression. "Overall," he notes, "the record of advances in the last decade ... — whether family life, schools, communities, employment, national service, or youth development — provides but a slim reed of hope for a better deal for much of the nation's youth and young families" (1998, p. I).

The intransigence of the conditions facing our most challenged children and young people underscores why resilience is such a galvanizing concept. In the decade since the seemingly radical view espoused in *Fostering Resiliency in Kids* — that the most effective, efficient, and even rewarding and joyful approach to problem prevention is through supporting healthy youth development — resilience has become much more accepted. Practitioners respond to its intuitive, common-sensical appeal. The prevention research community is heartened by the accumulating research evidence that resilience and youth development approaches work. As one leading researcher explains, "While part of the support for health promotion as a preventive strategy can be made on conceptual grounds, the major evidence is present in outcome studies.... In other words, *empirical data suggest that promoting health is one way to prevent later problems* [emphasis in the original]" (Durlak, 2000, p. 221; Masten & Coatsworth, 1998; Wyman, et al., 2000).

A few highlights of the last decade's resilience research and the resilience-focused youth development movement indicate how foundational and far-ranging this activity has been:

- Werner and Smith completed their longitudinal study of 700 "high-risk" children, following them to adulthood and midlife (ages 32 and 40).

- Several other longitudinal studies came of age: Clausen, 1993; Furstenberg et al., 1998; Hetherington & Kelly, 2002; Ryff et al., 1998; Vaillant, 2002.

- The MacArthur Foundation created the Research Network on Successful Adolescent Development Among Youth in High-Risk Settings.

- An interdisciplinary and cross-governmental-agency conference on the Role of Resilience in Mental Illness and Alcohol Abuse was convened.

- SAMHSA (Substance Abuse and Mental Health Services Administration) of the U.S. Department of Health and Human Services convened a "resilience working group" to inform funding initiatives.

- For the first time, a large-scale national survey of adolescent health included protective factors as well as risk factors (National Longitudinal Study of Adolescent Health).

- Many thoughtful qualitative studies of youth from culturally marginalized populations affirmed resilience theories.

- Program evaluations such as that of the Big Brothers Big Sisters mentoring program and the longitudinal follow-up of High/Scope's Perry Preschool Program supported resilience-based approaches.

- Journals in many fields (e.g., developmental psychopathology, school psychology, and clinical psychology) devoted special issues to the topic of resilience.

- The "positive psychology" movement was born.

- The Search Institute focused national attention on assets.

- The Asset-Based Community Development Institute was launched at Northwestern University.

- *Resiliency in Action* became the first journal devoted to the application of resilience research and theory.

- The Center for Youth Development and Policy Research under Karen Pittman's leadership began to support a national youth development movement.

- The International Youth Foundation and its Forum for Youth Investment (once again under Karen Pittman's leadership) began to support research and practice networks devoted to promoting positive youth development.

- Brain science began documenting the incredible lifelong plasticity of the human brain as well as its intensive early development.

In the pages that follow, no attempt has been made to be inclusive of the abundance of strengths-based research now available. Instead, the goal is to synthesize and integrate some of the key research findings and their application in programs and movements that support positive youth development and resilience. The emphases here on providing a framework, research support, and a rationale for resilience-based prevention and education are in line with

Practitioners respond to the intuitive, common-sensical approach of resilience-based programs.

the profound messages of long-term developmental studies of youth in high-risk environments:

(1) Resilience is a capacity all youth have for healthy development and successful learning.

(2) Certain personal strengths are associated with healthy development and successful learning.

(3) Certain characteristics of families, schools, and communities are associated with the development of personal strengths and, in turn, healthy development and successful learning.

(4) Changing the life trajectories of children and youth from risk to resilience starts with changing the beliefs of the adults in their families, schools, and communities.

Finally, *Resiliency: What We Have Learned* presents a perspective on resilience that calls for transformation of all our youth- and human-services systems. The challenge is not only to restructure policies and programs but to fundamentally alter relationships, beliefs, and power opportunities to focus on human capacities and gifts rather than on challenges and problems.

resilience: a universal capacity

CHAPTER 1

Resilience: A Universal Capacity

A consistent yet amazing finding over the last two decades of resilience research is that most children and youth, even those from highly stressed families or resource-deprived communities, do *somehow* manage to make decent lives for themselves. In fact, for just about any population of children that research has found to be at greater risk than normal for later problems — children who experience divorce, live with step-parents, lose a sibling, have attention deficit disorder, suffer developmental delays, become delinquent, run away, get involved with religious cults, and so on — more of these children make it than do not (Rhodes & Brown, 1991). In most studies, the figure seems to average 70 to 75 percent and includes children who were placed in foster care (Festinger, 1984), were members of gangs (Vigil, 1990), were born to teen mothers (Furstenberg, 1998), were sexually abused (Higgins, 1994; Wilkes, 2002; Zigler & Hall, 1989), had substance-abusing or mentally ill families (Beardslee, 1988; Chess, 1989; Watt, 1984; Werner, 1986; Werner & Smith, 2001), and grew up in poverty (Clausen, 1993; Schweinhart et al., 1993; Vaillant, 2002). In absolute worst case scenarios, when children experience multiple and persistent risks, still half of them overcome adversity and achieve good developmental outcomes (Rutter, 1987, 2000).

Researchers Emmy Werner and Ruth Smith, in their seminal study of risk and resilience, followed nearly 700 children growing up with risk factors (one-third of whom had multiple risk factors) from birth to adulthood. As the cohort of children aged, they grew increasingly more like their peers without risk factors (see Figure 1). Werner and Smith report, "One of the most striking findings of our two follow-ups in adulthood, at ages thirty-two and forty, was that most of the high-risk youths who did develop serious coping problems in adolescence had staged a recovery by the time they reached midlife.... They were in stable marriages and jobs, were satisfied with their relationships with their spouses and teenage children, and were responsible citizens in their community" (2001, p. 167). In fact, only one out of six of the adult subjects at either age 32 or 40 was doing poorly — "struggling with chronic financial problems, domestic conflict, violence, substance abuse, serious mental health problems, and/or low self-esteem" (2001, p. 37).

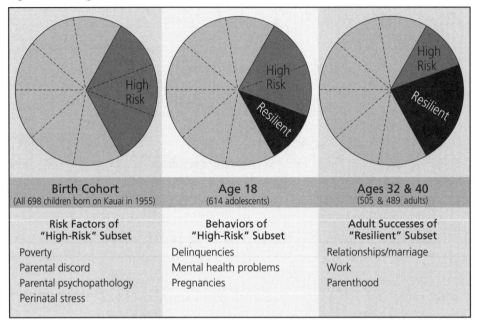

Birth Cohort	Age 18	Ages 32 & 40
(All 698 children born on Kauai in 1955)	(614 adolescents)	(505 & 489 adults)
Risk Factors of "High-Risk" Subset	**Behaviors of "High-Risk" Subset**	**Adult Successes of "Resilient" Subset**
Poverty	Delinquencies	Relationships/marriage
Parental discord	Mental health problems	Work
Parental psychopathology	Pregnancies	Parenthood
Perinatal stress		

These findings confound a core belief of many risk-focused social scientists — that risk factors for the most part predict negative outcomes. Instead, resilience research suggests that risk factors are predictive for only about 20 to 49 percent of a given high-risk population (Rutter, 1987, 2000; Werner, 2001). In contrast, "protective factors," the supports and opportunities that buffer the effect of adversity and enable development to proceed, appear to predict positive outcomes in anywhere from 50 to 80 percent of a high-risk population. According to Werner and Smith, "Our findings and those by other American and European investigators with a life-span perspective suggest that these buffers [i.e., protective factors] make a more profound impact on the life course of children who grow up under adverse conditions than do specific risk factors or stressful life events. They [also] appear to transcend ethnic, social class, geographical, and historical boundaries. Most of all, they offer us a more optimistic outlook than the perspective that can be gleaned from the literature on the negative consequences of perinatal trauma, caregiving deficits, and chronic poverty" (1992, p. 202).

Despite years of promising resilience research, popular myths about early adversity prevail. Ironically, the successful public relations campaign to highlight the importance of the first three years of life misrepresents some of the brain science that was its inspiration. Lost in the media blitz are the findings over this past decade pointing to the plasticity of the human brain (Bruer, 1999; Diamond & Hopson, 1998; Eriksson et al., 1998; Kagan, 1998). As Daniel Goleman notes in his discussion of the "protean brain," the "finding that the brain and nervous system generate new cells as learning or repeated experiences dictate has put the theme of *plasticity* [emphasis added] at the front and center of neuroscience" (2003, p. 334). Unfortunately, what the public has been left with instead, warns prominent developmental psychologist Jerome Kagan, is the "seductive" notion of "infant determinism" (1998).

Even among researchers and practitioners, the nature of resilience is commonly misunderstood. One misconception is the idea that resilience is a quality some people possess and others do not. Some researchers over the last decade have embarked on studies identifying "stress-resilient" and "stress-affected" children (Work et al., 1990), seeing resilience as a personality trait that one either has or does not have, rather than as an innate capacity bolstered by environmental protective factors. The popular press further distorts this limited understanding of resilience with stories about "invincible kids" (Brownlee, 1996), confirming many readers' beliefs that since some kids succeed no matter what, those who do not must somehow be at fault. A related misconception is that the findings from resilience research only apply to "high-risk youth." In fact, the supports and opportunities serving as protective factors for youth facing adversity apply equally to all young people. Distinctions between resiliency and concepts like "thriving" fail to recognize that resilience is itself normative.

The perpetuation of myths and misconceptions about resilience may well have its roots in a non-developmental, medical model of psychopathology that has dominated the field of social and behavioral sciences for decades. This deficit paradigm sees the proverbial glass as "half-empty." But as Werner and Smith explain, "[Resilience studies] provide us with a corrective lens — an awareness of the *self-righting tendencies* that move children toward normal adult development under all but the most persistent adverse circumstances" (1992, p. 202).

In fact, the powerful, simply stated message of *Fostering Resiliency in Kids* — that "The development of human resiliency is none other than the process of healthy human development" (Benard, 1991, p. 18) — has been borne out in this last decade of research. Ann Masten, one of today's premier resilience

> "Buffers [protective factors] make a more profound impact on the life course of children who grow up under adverse conditions than do specific risk factors or stressful life events. They appear to transcend ethnic, social class, geographical, and historical boundaries."
>
> — Emmy Werner & Ruth Smith

researchers, has taken the lead in advocating the position that resilience is a normative process of human adaptation, encoded in the human species and applicable to development in both favorable and unfavorable environments (2001, p. l; Masten & Coatsworth, 1998). According to Masten, "What began as a quest to understand the extraordinary has revealed the power of the ordinary. Resilience does not come from rare and special qualities, but from the everyday magic of ordinary, normative human resources in the minds, brains, and bodies of children, in their families and relationships, and in their communities" (Masten, 2001, p. 9). The innate self-righting tendencies and environmental protective factors that account for the resilience of young people facing adversity and challenge are precisely the same supports and opportunities that nurture us all.

As clear as it has become that all young people have the capacity for positive development, resilience research should never be used to justify social and political inaction on the grounds that, *somehow,* "Most kids make it." In the face of growing global poverty, abuse, violence, and other threats to children's development, the *somehow* can no longer depend on the luck of the draw. Increasingly, healthy youth development must depend on deliberate policies, practices, and interventions designed to provide young people with developmental supports and opportunities. As we are learning, young people are resilient, but they are not invincible.

personal strengths

CHAPTER 2

Resilience Outcomes: Personal Strengths

Personal resilience strengths are the individual characteristics, also called internal assets or personal competencies, associated with healthy development and life success. They do not cause resilience but rather are the positive developmental *outcomes* demonstrating that this innate capacity is engaged. Michael Baizerman, Professor of Youth Studies at the University of Minnesota, refers to this as "phenomenological resilience," that which can be seen, observed, and measured. Said even more simply, these personal strengths are what resilience looks like (see Figure 2).

Four categories of often overlapping personal strengths, or manifestations of resilience, were outlined ten years ago in *Fostering Resiliency in Kids* and labeled (1) social competence, (2) problem solving, (3) autonomy, and (4) sense of purpose. While researchers and writers often use differing names for these personal strengths, regardless of terminology, these categories hold up under the scrutiny of another decade of research. [Appendix A compares popular terms for these personal strengths across various theoretical perspectives.] In fact, as Masten states, "Recent studies continue to corroborate the importance of a relatively small set of global factors associated with resilience" (2001, p. 8) that are both personal and environmental. These competencies and strengths appear to transcend ethnicity, culture, gender, geography, and time (Werner & Smith, 1992, 2001). According to a National Research Council and Institute of Medicine report on youth development, "The little available evidence suggests that most of these characteristics are important in all cultural groups" (Eccles & Gootman, 2002, p. 81). Similarly, Werner and Smith find that they also are important across gender (1982, 1992, 2001). These resilience strengths are most fittingly seen as developmental possibilities that can be engaged in all individuals through the provision of the supports and opportunities discussed in chapters 4 through 8.

Figure 2. Personal Strengths: What Resilience Looks Like

SOCIAL COMPETENCE	PROBLEM SOLVING	AUTONOMY	SENSE OF PURPOSE
Responsiveness	Planning	Positive Identity	Goal Direction
			Achievement Motivation
Communication	Flexibility	Internal Locus of Control	Educational Aspirations
		Initiative	
Empathy	Resourcefulness		Special Interest
Caring		Self-Efficacy	Creativity
	Critical Thinking	Mastery	Imagination
Compassion	Insight		
Altruism		Adaptive Distancing	Optimism
Forgiveness		Resistance	Hope
		Self-Awareness	Faith
		Mindfulness	Spirituality
			Sense of Meaning
		Humor	

SOCIAL COMPETENCE

According to Luthar, "Developmental psychologists consider social competence to be a particularly useful indicator of children's overall positive adaptation or wellness" (Luthar & Burak, 2000, p. 30). Social competence includes the characteristics, skills, and attitudes essential to forming relationships and positive attachments to others. It runs the gamut from having an "easy" temperament to behaving altruistically. Daniel Goleman (1995) names social competence as one of the five ingredients of emotional intelligence. Referred to by Howard Gardner (1993) as "interpersonal intelligence," it is one of his seven original multiple intelligences.

Responsiveness

Foremost, social competence depends on the ability to elicit positive responses from others. Werner and Smith found this quality, which they refer to as "easy temperament," predictive of adult adaptation (1992, 2001). Wyman and his colleagues similarly found in the Rochester Child Resilience Project that characteristics of being "well-regulated" and "positive in mood" led to the responsiveness of others and predicted children's healthy adaptation (1991, 1999). Lillian Rubin's study of "transcendent" children referred to this quality as "adoptability" (1996), while Masten and Coatsworth (1998) use the terms "appealing" and "sociable." Wolin and Wolin, who identify relationship skills as one of their seven resiliencies, elaborate the process leading to mutually responsive relationships: "Early on, resilient children search out love by connecting or attracting the attention of available adults. Though the pleasures of connections are fleeting and often less than ideal, these early contacts seem enough to give resilient survivors a sense of their own appeal. Infused with confidence, they later branch out into active recruiting — enlisting a friend, neighbor, teacher, policeman, or minister as a parent substitute. Over time, recruiting rounds out to attaching, an ability to form and to keep mutually gratifying relationships" (1993, p. 111).

Communication

Social communication skills enable all of the processes of interpersonal connection and relationship building. A particular communication skill, the ability to assert oneself without violating others, is the basis of the conflict resolution/mediation programs that proliferated during the last decade, many with positive effects on reducing interpersonal conflict and other health-risk behaviors (Center for the Study and Prevention of Violence, n.d.; Englander-Golden, 1991; Englander-Golden et al., 1996, 2002).

Cross-cultural communication skills or cultural competence received much research attention over the last decade. For youth of non-dominant cultures, the ability to move back and forth between their primary culture and the dominant culture, or to accommodate the dominant culture without assimilating into it, means learning the "codes of power" while retaining their cultural and self identities. This ability has consistently been identified with school success and positive youth development outcomes (Delpit, 1995; Eccles & Gootman, 2002; Gibson, 1997a, b; Luthar & McMahon, 1996; Mehan et al., 1994). It has also been found to be related to less substance use among youth (Oetting, 1993).

code switching
dominant imposed?

Empathy and Caring

Empathy, the ability to know how another feels and understand another's perspective, is a hallmark of resilience (Werner, 1989; 1992). Empathy not only helps facilitate relationship development, it also helps form the basis of morality, forgiveness, and compassion and caring for others. It is "the fundamental people skill" according to Goleman's (1995) emotional intelligence work. He cites an international study of over 7,000 people that found "The benefits of being able to read feelings from nonverbal cues included being better adjusted emotionally, more popular, more outgoing, and more sensitive" (p. 97). Conversely, he states, "The lack of empathy is seen in criminal psychopaths, rapists, and child molesters" (p. 97). Empathy has been identified as a strong predictor of males' prosocial behavior (Roberts & Strayer, 1996). Moreover, the presence of empathy and caring was found to be a differentiating factor in Werner and Smith's 18-year-old resilient males (1982).

The Search Institute found some "disturbing trends" in their survey research related to the internal asset of empathy and caring. First, caring appears to diminish as youth grow older. While 61 percent of those in grades 6–8 report themselves as caring, only 46 percent of youth in grades 9–12 express this value. According to Peter Benson, "These numbers suggest that we graduate into adulthood a majority of youth who have lost…the values of caring and compassion" (1997, p. 48). This decline in empathy is especially true for males, with only about one-third of young men holding this value in grades 10–12.

Compassion, Altruism, and Forgiveness

Compassion is the desire and will to care for and to help alleviate another's suffering. It is a quality the positive psychology movement's *Values in Action Classification of Strengths* (Peterson & Seligman, 2003) refers to as humanity, which consists of both kindness and loving and being loved or, more simply, as loving kindness. Recent mind-body research has documented both physiological (immune system) and psychological health benefits from experiences of compassion (Rein et al., 1995).

Like compassion, altruism is often thought of as empathy in action. "The claim that feeling empathic emotion for someone in need evokes altruistic motivation to relieve that need has been called the empathy-altruism hypothesis" (Batson et al., 2002, p. 488). According to these positive psychologists, "Results of the over 25 experiments designed to test this hypothesis against various egoistic alternatives have proven remarkably supportive, leading to the tentative conclusion that feeling empathy for a person in need does indeed evoke altruistic motivation to help that person" (p. 494).

Altruism is not synonymous with helping, however. It refers more precisely to "doing for others what they need and not what you want to do for them" (Durlak, 2000; Vaillant, 2002, p. 71). While altruism is a purely unselfish form of helping, it does, in fact, rebound to the benefit of the helper and is considered the highest form of social competence, (Higgins, 1994; Oliner & Oliner, 1989). In his longitudinal study of adult development, Vaillant (2002) found altruism to be a "transformative" adaptive defense that turns lead into gold — even in the absence of environmental supports and opportunities.

While altruism is a purely unselfish form of helping, it does, in fact, rebound to the benefit of the helper.

Gina O'Connell Higgins (1994) documents this quality of compassion and altruism in most of her resilient adults who learned not only to love others but to help alleviate others' suffering — in spite of their own childhoods of severe deprivation and abuse. Werner and Smith (2001) also cite a longitudinal study of adults who were imprisoned as children with their mothers during the Greek Civil War (Dalianis, 1994), noting that "The most striking qualities shared by these child survivors in adulthood was their compassion for others in need" (p. 11).

Clear in all the resilience literature is the value of forgiveness of self and others, including even one's abusers. "In general, self-report measures of the propensity to forgive…are correlated positively…with measures of mental health and well-being" (McCullough & Witvliet, 2002, p. 451). Perhaps the most cited example of forgiveness is the story Robert Coles (1986) recounts of Ruby Bridges, the six-year-old African American girl who helped integrate the New Orleans public schools. Despite being spit on, cursed, jeered, and despised, she was able to forgive her tormentors by not taking personally their ignorance and racism.

PROBLEM-SOLVING SKILLS

This category encompasses many abilities, from planning and flexibility through resourcefulness, critical thinking, and insight. The glue that holds them together as a category is a figuring-things-out quality. Werner and Smith found that "Among the high risk individuals who succeeded against the odds, there was a significant association between…a nonverbal measure of problem-solving skills at age 10 and successful adaptation in adulthood" (1992, p. 176). This attribute is often referred to in resilience research as "good intellectual functioning" (Masten & Coatsworth, 1998).

Planning

Planning, as a form of problem solving, has been hypothesized to be the critical skill learned at age three or four in the High/Scope Educational Research Foundation's Perry Preschool Program. The planning children engaged in enabled their sense of control and hope for the future, thus facilitating broad, positive, adult life outcomes (Schweinhart et al., 1993; Schweinhart & Weikart, 1997a, b, c). Quinton and his associates (1993) found planful behavior was the primary internal asset of individuals that helped them to avoid choosing troubled mates. This study supported an earlier study (Rutter & Quinton, 1984) that also found planning in the choice of mates to be the critical attribute of institutionally reared women who overcame the odds to lead healthy and successful lives. Similarly, John Claussen's (1993) longitudinal study of children growing up in the Great Depression found that "planful competence" in adolescence predicted greater educational attainment and fewer life crises in every decade up to their fifties. For the men it predicted greater occupational attainment and for the women happier and more lasting marriages.

Flexibility

Flexibility, another problem-solving skill, entails the ability to see alternatives and attempt alternative solutions to both cognitive and social problems. It includes the ability to change courses and not to get stuck. *Aging Well,* George Vaillant's (2002) book about Harvard University's more than 50 years of research on healthy and successful adult development, documents that adaptive coping, another form of flexibility, is a critical life skill. Similarly, in the last decade, the author has asked thousands of adults what personal strength has helped them deal with stress and challenge; flexibility is one of the most often named personal resources. It is also one of the foci of current conflict resolution programs (Crawford & Bodine, 1996).

Resourcefulness

Resourcefulness, a critical survival skill, involves identifying external resources and surrogate sources of support. It is a skill also referred to as help-seeking, resource utilization, and just plain "street smarts." Werner and Smith (1992) found this a critical survival skill that connected challenged youth with environmental resources. Gina O'Connell Higgins (1994), who reviewed the lives of adults who had been sexually abused as children, also documents how valuable this strength was in connecting to turnaround people and places. Of course, resourcefulness must be followed up with initiative, with actually reaching out to available supports and opportunities (see page 22 and the discussion of internal locus of control and initiative). The skill of resourcefulness was found to be an essential component in early intervention programs supporting children growing up in alcoholic families (Beardslee, 1997).

Critical Thinking and Insight

Critical thinking refers to higher-order thinking skills, analytic habits of thinking that go beneath surface impressions, traditional myths, and opinions to an understanding of the context or to discovering the deep meaning of any event, statement, or situation (Schor, 1993). It can also include meta-learning skills, that is, learning how to learn, or meta-cognitive skills that allow one to examine one's own thought process (this is similar to what is described as self-awareness on page 26). Meta-cognitive skills include problem-solving appraisal (Heppner & Lee, 2002), and, according to researchers of this concept, problem-solving appraisal strengths are associated with better psychological and social adjustment, lower levels of depression and anxiety, greater hope, better physical health, and better coping with adversity (Heppner & Lee).

Critical thinking helps young people develop a sense of critical consciousness, the awareness of the structures of oppression (whether imposed by an alcoholic parent, an insensitive school, or a racist society, for example) and the creation of strategies for overcoming them, helping, thus, to prevent internalized oppression and a sense of victimhood (Freire, 1993; hooks, 1994).

Insight is the deepest form of problem solving and very similar to the concept of critical consciousness. It includes intuitive awareness of environmental cues — especially of danger — as well as realizations that transform one's perceived reality. According to Wolin and Wolin (1993), insight is the personal strength that contributes most to resiliency. They define it as "the mental habit of asking penetrating questions of oneself and, subsequently, providing honest answers" (p. 71). In her qualitative study of resilient children from troubled families, Lillian Rubin describes those able to use insight as follows: "They make their way comfortably in the social world while, at the same time, they move about that world with a healthy skepticism, rarely falling victim to naïve assumptions, always wary about accepting what they see around them at face value — a product, no doubt, of having grown up in an environment where the façade of family and social life was very different from the reality" (1996, p. 224).

Insight allows children growing up in great adversity to figure out that all fathers do not beat their children, that a schizoprenic mother's bizarre behavior is not normal, that many children do have enough food to eat and a safe place to sleep, etc. Insight helps children interpret and perceive their adversity in a way that allows them to move beyond victimhood and see themselves and their lives in new ways (O'Gorman, 1994). Insight is demonstrated, for example, when children growing up in troubled families "see themselves as different from their parents; remain relatively free of guilt because a parent's illness cannot be a child's fault; filter and evaluate the information disturbed parents

Insight allows children growing up in great adversity to figure out that all fathers do not beat their children, that a schizoprenic mother's bizarre behavior is not normal, that many children do have enough food to eat and a safe place to sleep, etc.

pass along; and hold images of themselves and of the world they inhabit that are more pleasing than the ones their parents project" (Wolin & Wolin, 1993, p. 79). Lillian Rubin's study of "transcendent" adults includes the following description of the development of her own sense of insight: "In my own life, although my mother kept telling me that my brother was the smart one in the family, my teachers reflected back another image of myself. Where my mother was rejecting, they were kind and accepting; where she told me I wasn't smart, they let me know I was. It didn't take the sting of my mother's rejection away, but it did open up the possibility of another way of seeing myself that I could take comfort in" (Beneke, 1997, p. 10).

Like other resilience strengths, psychologists increasingly believe that insight is not just something we use "when confronted with perplexing obstacles. On the contrary, humans seek out problems to be solved; solving problems is one of our great joys" (Schulman, 2002, p. 322). In fact, Schulman's research on children as young as two years old finds that even they are driven by four basic questions: "What's out there? What leads to what? What makes things happen? and What's controllable?" (p. 322).

AUTONOMY

The category of autonomy includes many inter-related and overlapping sub-categories of attributes revolving around the development of one's sense of self, of identity, and of power. Autonomy involves an ability to act independently and to feel a sense of control over one's environment. Gordon and Song's (1994) retrospective qualitative study of successful African Americans who were raised in poverty found autonomy, or self-directedness, a common strength. In the field of motivational psychology, Deci and Ryan's more than 30 years of research on self-determination theory has documented autonomy as the critical personal strength underlying other strengths and intrinsic motivation. They state, in fact, that "feelings of competence [in any skill or task] will not enhance intrinsic motivation unless accompanied by a sense of autonomy…." (Ryan & Deci, 2000, p. 70). This finding has profound implications for teaching and learning, as we will see in our discussion of engaging schools.

Autonomy is also associated with positive health and a sense of well-being (Deci, 1995; Ryan & Deci, 2000). "To be autonomous means to act in accord with one's self — it means feeling free and volitional in one's actions. When autonomous, people are fully willing to do what they are doing, and they embrace the activity with a sense of interest and commitment. Their actions emanate from their true sense of self" (Deci, 1995, p. 2).

Positive Identity

According to Erik Erikson's (1968) theory of psychosocial development, achievement of a positive, coherent identity — the sense of one's internal, relatively stable self apart from others — is the critical developmental task of adolescence. Harter concurs: "Defining who one is in relation to multiple others, determining what one will become, and discovering which of one's many selves is the 'true self' are the normative developmental tasks of this period" (1990, p. 383). Adams and his colleagues explain further, "Not yet firmly tied by adult commitments, the adolescent may try out a variety of commitments in occupation and ideology, eventually adopting a more or less permanent sense of who he or she is" (1992, p. 10).

Research has confirmed that a clear sense of identity is associated with optimal psychological functioning in terms of personal well-being and the absence of anxiety and depression; with goal-directed activity and problem solving; and with social competence, in terms of attitudes of social acceptance, cooperation and helping, and intimate personal relationships (Waterman, 1992). Positive self-identity is closely aligned and often used synonymously with positive self-evaluation or self-esteem. These characteristics are not only critical to normative development but have consistently been documented as characteristics describing "resilient" children and adolescents, those who have overcome many odds (Masten & Coatsworth, 1998; Werner & Smith, 1992).

Research in this last decade has also looked at the concept of social identities, identities related to one's membership in a social group. "For adolescents from ethnic minority groups, the process of identity formation has an added dimension due to their exposure to alternative sources of identification, their own ethnic group and the mainstream or dominant culture" (Phinney & Rosenthal, 1992, p. 145). Furthermore, according to Phinney and Rosenthal, "If ethnic minority youth are to construct a strong, positive, and stable self-identity, then they must be able to incorporate into that sense of self a positively valued ethnic identity" (p. 145).

While much research, especially longitudinal, still needs to be done, according to a National Research Council and Institute of Medicine report, "Recent studies have found that having a strong positive ethnic identity is associated with having high self-esteem, a strong commitment to doing well in school, a strong sense of purpose in life, great confidence in one's own personal efficacy, and high academic achievement" (Eccles & Gootman, 2002, p. 80).

Recent studies have found that a strong positive ethnic identity is associated with high self-esteem, a strong commitment to doing well in school, a strong sense of purpose in life, great confidence in one's own efficacy, and high academic achievement.

Internal locus of control

has long been associated

with better health

habits, compliance,

and fewer illnesses.

Neighborhood-based organizations that provide youth the opportunity to explore their ethnic identities as well as those of others have been found to be a major source of support for adolescents in developing a positive sense of self (Heath & McLaughlin, 1993; McLaughlin et al., 1994).

Internal Locus of Control and Initiative

Internal locus of control, a generalized sense of being in charge or of having personal power, was a key determinant of resilience in Werner and Smith's (1992) longitudinal study, in the Rochester Longitudinal Study (Wyman et al., 1992), and in the life-course study conducted by Norman Watt and his colleagues (1995). In the latter, 78 percent of these resilient adults agreed that "A primary requirement for transcending adversity…was to understand that they were able to control the course of their lives" (p. 233).

In a review of empowerment, Wallerstein states, "People with an internal locus of control have long been associated with better health habits, compliance, and fewer illnesses than those with an external locus of control" (1992, p. 199). While studies continually find an association between lack of control and depression (Seligman, 1992), a recent study also found that a sense of personal control explained most of the relationship between socioeconomic status and depression (Turner et al., 1999). Luthar and Zigler (1992) also found in their study of inner-city youth that believing "that events in their lives are determined largely by their own efforts" was associated with their motivation and effort to do well at school, a finding also of the earlier work of Jeff Howard and the Efficacy Institute (1992).

Recent research on HIV-positive men has revealed that even an *unrealistic* sense of personal control is health protective (Taylor et al., 2000). Making the case that the control motive is basic to the human condition, Thompson (2002) cites research studies that have demonstrated its many benefits: better ability to deal with stress, less anxiety and depression, less traumatization by victimization, and more initiative and better physical health. Conversely, powerlessness — external locus of control or learned helplessness (acting like a victim) — has a long history in stress research, experimental psychology, social psychology, and social epidemiology as a major risk factor for disease (Herman, 1997; Ryan & Deci, 2000; Seligman, 1992/1998; Wallerstein, 1992).

One important caution in looking at internal locus of control is that the development of this quality rests on individuals first recognizing what they *cannot* control, that is, what is outside of their "sphere of influence" (Stohlberg

& Mahler, 1994). For example, children must recognize that the abuse they've experienced at home or the racism they encountered in their school was not their fault and was not within their sphere of influence or control.

According to Higgins, recognizing prior victimization actually leads to heightening one's internal locus of control. "Once you see what you could not possibly control as a child, you can also honor what you are able to control in adulthood — primarily yourself and your own reactions to external events" (1994, p. 293). She goes on to observe that "The resilient resolve to put their fate in their own hands. To do this, they are willing to take great — although carefully calculated — risks to reshape their lot. They find the role of adult victim frightening, since it gives away power and control to others" (p. 294).

Initiative, a concept almost synonymous with locus of control, is defined by Larson as the "ability to be motivated from within to direct attention and effort toward a challenging goal" (2000, p. 170). Erikson (1968) saw the development of initiative as the critical task of childhood. Initiative, in terms of the action step that follows identifying resources and believing you can connect with them, is often labeled support-seeking in community psychology (Barrera & Prelow, 2000) or recruiting by clinical psychologists (Higgins, 1994; Wolin & Wolin, 1993). Vaillant found this quality to be one that differentiated healthy development across the lifespan. Resilient adults, he notes, "don't nurse resentments or the poor-me's, but ask for help" (2002, p. 308).

Larson claims that initiative is a core quality of positive youth development in Western culture and lies at the heart of other strengths such as creativity, leadership, altruism, and civic engagement. He sees initiative not only as the action of engaging resources but of engaging in a concentrated activity, similar to Csikszentmihalyi's (1990) concept of "flow" (see a further discussion of flow on page 29, under special interest, creativity, and imagination).

Self-Efficacy and Mastery

Bandura's 20 years of research on self-efficacy has documented that it is the *belief* in one's power that determines personal life outcomes, no matter whether one actually has power (1995, 1997). According to another researcher, "Believing that you can accomplish what you want to accomplish is one of the most important ingredients — perhaps the most important ingredient — in the recipe for success" (Maddux, 2002, p. 277). In fact, "The timeless message of research on self-efficacy is the simple, powerful truth that confidence, effort, and persistence are more potent than innate ability" (p. 285).

Believing that events in their lives are determined largely by their own efforts was associated with inner-city youths' motivation and effort to do well at school.

During the last 15 years, much research has found that perceived self-efficacy is a critical factor in whether individuals change a whole range of health-risk behaviors (Schwarzer & Fuchs, 1995). "Perceived self-efficacy stands out as a major contributor [in adopting positive health behaviors] that affects not only the decision-making process but also the initiation and maintenance process" (Schwarzer & Fuchs, 1995, p. 281). In fact, all the major theories of health behavior include self-efficacy as a key component. According to Madux, "Researchers have shown that enhancing self-efficacy beliefs is crucial to successful change and maintenance of virtually every behavior crucial to health, including exercise, diet, stress management, safe sex, smoking cessation, overcoming alcohol abuse, compliance with treatment and prevention regimens, and disease detection behaviors such as breast self-examinations" (2002, p. 281).

Similarly, perceived self-efficacy plays a major role in educational success, in terms of both motivation and achievement. "The overall findings of cross-sectional, longitudinal, and experimental studies are quite consistent in showing that beliefs in personal efficacy enhance effort and persistence in academic activities" (Multon et al., 1991; Schunk, 1991; Zimmerman, 1995, p. 207). Not surprisingly, research has also demonstrated the impact of efficacy beliefs on actual academic achievement (Schunk, 1989).

Closely related to self-efficacy is mastery, which refers to feeling competent or experiencing the sense of doing something well. In fact, having mastery experiences is one of the most effective means of developing a sense of efficacy.

Experiences of overcoming challenges — whether intellectual or personal, help people recognize their resilience. According to Bandura, "After people become convinced they have what it takes to succeed, they persevere in the face of adversity and quickly rebound from setbacks. By sticking it out through tough times, they emerge stronger from adversity" (1995, p. 3). This statement is borne out in resilience studies again and again as a critical determinant of life success (Masten & Coatsworth, 1998; Rutter, 1989; Werner & Smith, 1992). According to Masten (2002), mastery is a powerful motivational system, serving to keep development on course. This researcher has asked thousands of people over the last ten years the following question: "What has fostered your resilience; what has helped you see yourself and your life in a new way?" One of the most common responses refers to adversity and challenge. Respondents learned that they could, indeed, mend stronger at the break.

Adaptive Distancing and Resistance

Much has been written about the protective power of adaptive distancing for children growing up in families troubled by parental alcoholism, abuse, and mental illness. Adaptive distancing involves emotionally detaching oneself from parental, school, or community dysfunction, realizing that one is not the cause of and cannot control the dysfunction of others and that one's own future will be different (Beardslee, 1997; Beardslee & Podorefsky, 1988; Chess, 1989; Rubin, 1996). According to Chess, "Such distancing provided a buffer that was protective of developmental course, of self-esteem, and of the ability to acquire constructive goals" (1989, p. 195). Rubin saw this quality in the lives she studied as follows: "The ability to hold onto a self, even in the face of the assaults they suffered — made it possible to stand back and observe the fray without getting bogged down in it. They may have been pained, angered, and frightened by the events of their lives, but they retained enough distance not to get caught in endlessly blaming themselves" (1996, p. 225).

Resistance is one form of adaptive distancing. The refusal to accept negative messages about one's self, one's gender, or one's culture or race serves as a powerful protector of autonomy. A whole literature on "oppositional identity work" emerged in the 1990s to describe the strategies of resistance that marginalized youth use "to protect what they regard as their true selves" (Hemmings, 2000). Herb Kohl's (1994) essay, "I Won't Learn From You," narrates how resistance, while usually perceived negatively by schools and juvenile authorities, can be a powerful ally when working with marginalized young people. While resistance appears to be an internal protective mechanism guarding a person's sense of self, it requires the complementary development of a critical consciousness, insight, or self-awareness to become a positive, transformative strength.

Mehan and his colleagues found academically successful Latino and African American students employed a resistance strategy they refer to as "accommodation without assimilation" (1994, p. 113). These young people negotiated dual identities by achieving academically at school while affirming their cultural identity and maintaining a critical consciousness. Gordon and Song (1994) found their resilient adults had been able to withstand peer pressure to be part of gangs, to gamble, and so on, and to "march to the beat of a different drummer." When this quality of physical and emotional distancing is examined more closely, researchers have found it undergirded by self-awareness and mindfulness (see below). Weinstein (2002, p. 193) cites research by Mavis Sanders who found successful African American students

> **Refusal to accept negative messages about one's self, gender, or culture or race serves as a powerful protector of autonomy.**

reframed racism as a challenge, employing an "I'll show them" response which motivated their learning and life success: "All my life, I have hated to hear anyone say, 'You can't do this.' If someone tells me that I can't, I just find a way to do it. It makes me want to do it more" (Sanders, 1997, p. 90).

Self-Awareness and Mindfulness

Self-awareness, according to Daniel Goleman, is the most critical source of emotional intelligence. He defines self-awareness as "a nonreactive, nonjudgmental attention to inner states," sometimes called mindfulness (1995, pp. 47, 315). Jon Kabat-Zinn, perhaps the leading writer on mindfulness practice, sees mindfulness as "the art of conscious living…. It is simply a practical way to be more in touch with the fullness of our being through a systematic process of self-observation, self-inquiry, and mindful action…. It has to do with waking up and seeing things as they are" (1994, p. 6). "When we are mindful, we become sensitive to context and perspective; we are situated in the present" (Langer, 2002, p. 214). According to Shapiro and her colleagues (2002), mindfulness qualities consist of the following: nonjudging, nonstriving, acceptance, patience, trust, openness, letting go, gentleness, generosity, empathy, gratitude, and loving kindness. These qualities also comprise what Herbert Benson (1996) considers the "relaxation response," the innate capacity to tap into an inner source of peace. Thought/mood/affect recognition are other terms commonly used in the literature (Pransky, 1998; Vaillant, 2000).

Self-awareness includes observing one's thinking, feelings, attributions or "explanatory" style as well as paying attention to one's moods, strengths, and needs as they arise, without getting caught up in emotion. According to Goleman, "At a minimum, it manifests itself simply as a slight stepping-back from experience, a parallel stream of consciousness that is 'meta': hovering above or beside the main flow, aware of what is happening rather than being immersed and lost in it. It is the difference between being murderously enraged at someone and having the self-reflexive thought, 'This is anger I'm feeling' even as you are enraged" (1995, p. 47).

Over the course of 30 years' research with resilient children growing up in families with mental illness or their own physical illness, Beardslee found that self-understanding, "the capacity to reflect on one's surroundings," was what allowed them to adaptively distance and "take appropriate action." For example, Beardslee reports that those children he studied whose parents were ill "were able to articulate their difficulties at length and showed much awareness of their parents' disorder. At the same time, they saw themselves as separate from their parents' illness and fully comprehended that they were not to blame and should not feel guilty about it. They attributed their ability to move on and take action outside the home in part to this understanding" (1997, p. 525).

According to one of the developers of the theory of emotional intelligence, John Mayer, self-aware people "have some sophistication about their emotional lives. Their clarity about emotions may underlie other personality traits: they are autonomous and sure of their own boundaries, are in good psychological health, and tend to have a positive outlook on life. When they get into a bad mood, they don't ruminate and obsess about it, and are able to get out of it sooner. In short, their mindfulness helps them manage their emotions" (Goleman, 1995, p. 48). The capacity for self-awareness serves as a powerful self-regulatory, adaptational system "keeping development on course and facilitating recovery from adversity when more normative conditions are restored" (Masten, 2002, p. 82).

Self-awareness often involves not only stepping back from the grip of emotion, but the mental act of reframing (also referred to as cognitive restructuring) one's experience, to see oneself and one's life in new ways. Some thinkers consider this transformative, reframing power to be the essence of resilience (Beardslee, 1997; Benard & Marshall, 1997; Bennett-Goleman, 2001; Dalai Lama, 1998; Frankl, 1984; Kumpfer, 1999; Mills, 1995; O'Gorman, 1994; Salzberg, 2002; Vaillant, 2000; Wolin & Wolin, 1993).

Viktor Frankl saw evidence of this reframing power over and over in his years in concentration camps in Nazi Germany. He wrote, "We who lived in concentration camps can remember the men who walked through the huts comforting others, giving away their last piece of bread. They may have been few in number, but they offer sufficient proof that everything can be taken from a man but one thing: the last of the human freedoms — to choose one's attitude in any given set of circumstances, to choose one's own way" (1984, p. 86).

Humor

Besides serving as a powerful social competence skill helping to build positive connections between people (Lefcourt, 2001), humor helps one transform anger and sadness into laughter and helps one get distance from pain and adversity. Dacher Kelter's research on the differing effects of trauma on people's lives puts laughter high on the list of what can bring about meaning and positive transformation after a traumatic event. "Humans have a wonderful capacity to find humor in the juxtaposition of life and death. Many

> Self-awareness often involves not only stepping back from the grip of emotion, but the mental act of reframing one's experience, to see oneself and one's life in new ways. Some thinkers consider this transformative, reframing power to be the essence of resilience.

of our positive emotions are directed at transforming the distress and trauma that results from the human condition" (McBroom, 2002). Others also make the case for humor's ability to transform pain, for example in the midst of stress and challenge (Higgins, 1994; Kumpfer, 1999; Vaillant, 2000; Vande Berg & Van Bockern, 1995; Wolin & Wolin, 1993).

Higgins (1994) found in her research that healthy adults who had been sexually abused as children identified humor "as the polestar of their finding true pleasure despite their earlier agony. It is an aspect of them that they always engage, a part they always cherish.... It allows them to attain, as adults, some sense of [their lost] childhood" (p. 311). Likewise, Vaillant found humor to be one of the critical adaptive/mature defenses used by resilient individuals across the lifespan: "Mature humor allows people to look directly at what is painful…and permits the expression of emotion without individual discomfort and without unpleasant effects on others" (2000, p. 95).

A large research base establishes the power of humor even to physically heal (Lefcourt, 2002). Dr. Carl O. Simonton reports that "A 'lightness of being' — an ability to laugh, to play, or even simply to smile — can pull us out of despair and enlarge our wish to live by increasing the energy available for healing and recovery" (Burger, 1995, p. 15). Several studies over the last two decades have documented humor's positive effects on immune system functioning and, over the last decade, on its effect on neuroendocrine hormones involved in stress responses (Lefcourt, 2002).

A SENSE OF PURPOSE AND BRIGHT FUTURE

This category of inter-related strengths ranges from goal direction to optimism to creativity to a sense of meaning and coherence — the deep belief that one's life has meaning and that one has a place in the universe. These assets, based on an orientation toward a compelling and bright future, are probably the most powerful in propelling young people to healthy outcomes despite adversity (Werner & Smith, 1982, 1992). A positive and strong future focus has consistently been identified with academic success, a positive self-identity, and fewer health-risk behaviors (Masten & Coatsworth, 1998; Quinton et al., 1993; Seligman, 2002; Snyder et al., 2002; Wyman et al., 1993).

Goal Direction, Achievement Motivation, and Educational Aspirations

All of these future-oriented resilience strengths are attributed in the literature to young people who succeed in school (Anderman et al., 2002) and who do *not* get in trouble with alcohol and other drugs, with teen pregnancy, or with dropping out of school, even in the face of multiple risks and challenges (Wiglield & Eccles, 2002; Furstenberg et al., 1998; Masten, 1994; Newcomb & Bentler, 1988; Watt et al., 1995; Werner & Smith, 1992). Goal-direction is also synonymous with planful competence, discussed earlier as a problem-solving skill. Higgins found that a "fierce fidelity to a nascent vision" enabled her challenged youths to persevere during their traumatic childhoods (1994, p. 124). Similarly, Watt and his colleagues used terms such as "relentless effort," "persistent inner drive," and "unshakable determination to survive" as the critical attributes in their longitudinal study of resilience (1995, p. 240). Such "anticipation," defined by Vaillant (2000) as going beyond cognitive planning to also feeling about the future, is yet another adaptive mechanism contributing to health and wellness. The more general concept of intrinsic motivation, of having direction, persistence, determination, and intention, is also used by motivational psychologists to describe optimal human functioning (Ryan & Deci, 2000).

A positive and strong future focus has consistently been identified with academic success, a positive self-identity, and fewer health-risk behaviors.

Achievement motivation is one of the key factors influencing behavior and performance. It "refers to motivation in situations in which individuals' competence is at issue" (Wigfield & Eccles, 2002, p. 1). According to a literature review by Scales and Leffert (1999), achievement motivation has been consistently linked to academic success factors, such as increased high school completion, increased enrollment in college, increased reading and mathematics achievement test scores, and higher grades. Moreover, they also found achievement motivation associated with better mental health, communication skills, and lower levels of problem behaviors. In a 1992 analysis of two longitudinal studies, High School and Beyond (HS&B) and the National Educational Longitudinal Study of 1988 (NELS: 88), Peng (1994) found the individual factors of educational aspirations and internal locus of control to be the most powerful correlates of school success. Even in late life, according to Vaillant, "Gusto for education [remains] highly correlated with psychological health (2002, p. 246).

Special Interest, Creativity, and Imagination

Werner and Smith (1982, 1992) found that children who had special interests and hobbies that compelled their attention and gave them a sense of task mastery were among their resilient overcomers. "Most of the resilient children in our high-risk sample were not unusually talented, but they took great pleasure in interests and hobbies that brought them solace when things fell apart in their home lives" (1992, p. 205).

Resilience research

documents the critical

role that creativity

and imagination

play in surviving and

transcending adversity,

trauma, and risk.

This special interest is often in some form of the creative arts — painting, drawing, singing, playing music, dancing, drama, etc. The value for children of expressing creativity is validated by a growing body of research on the creative arts (Catterall, 1997; Heath et al., 1998; Morrison Institute, 1995), brain science (Diamond & Hopson, 1998; Sylwester, 1998), and multiple intelligences (H. Gardner, 1993, 2000). Resilience research documents the critical role that creativity and imagination play in surviving and transcending adversity, trauma, and risk (A. Miller, 1990; Higgins, 1994; Wolin & Wolin, 1993). Conversely, creativity research has demonstrated the relationship between later creativity and earlier adversity. According to Dean Keith Simonton, a leading creativity researcher, "It is a startling testimony to the adaptive powers of the human being that some of the most adverse childhoods can give birth to the most creative adulthoods" (2000, p. 153). Moreover, studies of successful aging also demonstrate the link between creativity in childhood and adolescence and psychological and physical well-being in adulthood (Csikszentmihalyi, 1996; Vaillant, 2002).

The imagination provides a channel to a positive future for children living in stressful environments (Rubin, 1996). For example, children's literature had been important to many in O'Connell Higgins study of resilient adults. "Books, the most accessible source of imagery during my subjects' childhoods in the forties and fifties, were especially pivotal to virtually *all* of them. Hungry readers from early on, they found in literature an omnipresent, movable feast. Authors often write to communicate their own vision, and many children feel that an author is writing to them personally. Thus many subjects said that literature provided deeply influential and satisfying company (1994, p. 179).

Having a special interest and being able to use one's creativity or imagination can result in "flow" or self-actualizing, optimal experiences, described earlier as experiences of total involvement, engagement, and participation. These flow experiences not only provide a sense of task mastery but offer a meaningful, compelling, transcendent experience, distancing one from current challenges and stresses and serving "as a buffer against adversity and prevent[ing] pathology" (Nakamura & Csikszentmihalyi, 2002, p. 102). As Csikszentmihalyi describes a flow experience, "Concentration is so intense that there is no attention left over to think about anything irrelevant, or to worry about problems. Self-consciousness disappears, and the sense of time becomes distorted. An activity that produces such experiences is so gratifying that people are willing to do it for its own sake, with little concern for what they will get out of it, even when it is difficult or dangerous" (1990, p. 71).

Csikszentmihalyi's years of research on flow support findings "by psychologists who study happiness, life satisfaction, and intrinsic motivation; by sociologists who see in [flow] the opposite of anomie and alienation; and by anthropologists who are interested in the phenomena of collective effervescence and rituals" (1990, p. 5). They have all found optimal experiences to be discriminating between people who experience a sense of psychological well-being and those who do not. In his study of "talented teens," Csikszentmihalyi and his colleagues (1994) found the nurturing of these experiences critical in adolescents who maintained their motivation and talents during the teen years.

Optimism and Hope

While optimism and hope each reflects a positive motivational stance and expectations toward the future, optimism is often linked to positive beliefs and cognitions, and hope is associated with positive emotions and feelings. Long-term studies of resilience as well as mind-body studies have found optimism and hope — usually referred to interchangeably in this literature — to be associated with holistic health: mental, physical, social, emotional, and spiritual (H. Benson, 1996; Carver & Scheier, 2002; Higgins, 1994; Peterson & Steen, 2002; Seligman, 1992/1998, 2002; Seligman et al., 1995; Snyder, 2000; Snyder et al., 2002; Werner & Smith, 1992, 2001).

Over the last decade, the influential psychologist Martin Seligman turned his research attention from depression and "learned helplessness" to optimism, strengths, and resilience (Seligman, 1992/1998, 2002; Seligman et al., 1995), mirroring and perhaps accelerating the paradigm shift taking place in the field generally. Seligman's research on optimism has focused on explanatory style, on how a person explains the causes of bad events. It goes a step beyond the self-awareness and mindfulness of recognizing one's thoughts and their role in creating one's reality to the act of choosing to see the glass as half-full instead of half-empty or to say "yes" instead of "no." Seligman and his colleagues found that the optimists they studied explained bad events in three very different ways from the pessimists:

	PESSIMIST	OPTIMIST
Personal:	"This is my fault."	"We're all doing the best we can."
Pervasive:	"My whole life is rotten."	"School is a challenge, but I love poetry."
Permanent:	"I'll always be a loser."	"Tomorrow I'm going to win."

Seligman's Penn Resiliency Project (Seligman et al., 1995), formerly called the Penn Prevention Project, takes the teaching of explanatory style down into the elementary grades. Children and youth were found to have less emotional distress and less physical illness after being part of this project (Peterson & Seligman, 2003). Others have found that even unrealistically optimistic beliefs about the future are health protective (Taylor et al., 2000).

With regard to the related concept of hope, Werner and Smith (1992, 2001) found that "The central component in the lives of the resilient individuals in this study which contributed to their effective coping in adulthood appeared to be a confidence [a hopefulness] that the odds can be surmounted." In Werner's three historical accounts of how children coped during the American Civil War (1998), as members of the Donner party crossing the High Sierras (1995), and during the London bombing raids during World War II (2000b), hope appears to have been the mainstay of these survivors. Higgins found hope so central in the lives of her survivors of childhood abuse, poverty, and cultural hatred that she frames her subjects' personal strengths and environmental supports and opportunities in terms of their "locus of hope."

In their studies of hope, positive psychologists have developed a "full hope model." According to these psychologists, "Hopeful thinking necessitates both the perceived capacity to envision workable routes [pathways] and goal-directed energy" (Snyder et al., 2002, p. 258). Not surprisingly, this research has shown direct connections between hope and the resilience strengths discussed above — social competence, problem solving, and self-efficacy, as well as with academic achievement.

Faith, Spirituality, and Sense of Meaning

This group of personal strengths represents the transformational quality of making meaning, whether by attributing meaning to that outside of one's control or by creating one's own meaning. It has been associated with healthy development throughout the lifespan.

Researchers have found that some resilient individuals draw strength from religion, others benefit from more general faith or spirituality, and others achieve a sense of stability or coherence by finding personal answers to questions about their sense of purpose and self-worth. According to Robert Coles (1990), "Children try to understand not only what is happening to them but why; and in doing that they call upon the religious life they have experienced, the spiritual values they have received, as well as other sources of potential explanation" (p. 100).

Having a belief system that allows one to attribute meaning to misfortune and illness, a form of reframing, has been found in mind-body medicine to produce better psychological and physical outcomes (O'Leary & Ickovics, 1995; Taylor et al., 2000). Other research has found that people who can attribute a spiritual design or meaning to personal adversity, tragedy, or trauma fare better psychologically — with less depression and anxiety — and physically (Masten, 1994; Gordon & Song, 1994; Pargament, 1997; Pargament & Mahoney, 2002).

"Religiosity," the importance of religious faith (but not necessarily of attending services), has been found to correlate with health-risk behavior reduction. The National Longitudinal Study of Adolescent Health (Resnick et al., 1997) found that for both middle and high school students, religiosity was associated with noninvolvement in health-risk behaviors of substance use, early sexual debut, and unsafe sex. This finding is also borne out in surveys done by the Search Institute (Benson et al., 1997; Donohue & Benson, 1995). Donohue and Benson (1995) found that by promoting altruism, religiosity likely had its greatest effect in protecting against risk behaviors.

However, religiosity was not found to be universally beneficial (Maton & Wells, 1995). In fact, Benson and his colleagues (1997) report that some religious approaches were found to be harmful. "Faith with an accepting and liberating message appeared to be associated with less antisocial behavior and more prosocial behavior among youth, whereas faith that had a controlling and rigid orientation seemed to be associated with young people's antisocial behavior" (Scales & Leffert, 1999, p. 162).

The poet and social critic Paul Goodman once said, "Faith is the knowledge that the ground will be there when you take a step" (Guy, 2003, p. 80). In her study of resilient adults, Higgins reports that most of them had as children found faith, regardless of religion. Drawing on faith development theory, (a developmental psychology approach to studying religion), she paraphrases Sharon Parks's definition of faith: "Convictional knowing...that in which we invest our hearts, the anchor which is adequate to ground, unify, and order our lives" (1994, p. 173). Higgins organizes this meaning-making process in terms of "two overarching themes: faith in surmounting and faith in human relationships as the wellspring of overcoming" (p. 172). "First," she suggests, "the resilient develop a core convictional foundation about the importance of loving well that withstands their harsh treatment as children. Second, their faith undergirds whatever specific religious or secular beliefs they might hold. Third, their faith is anchored in their relationships with others" (p. 173).

Some resilient individuals draw strength from religion, others benefit from more general faith or spirituality, and others achieve a sense of stability or coherence by finding personal answers to questions about their sense of purpose and self-worth.

Sharon Salzberg explains the beginning of her journey to "faith" or "core conviction" as follows: "My new story was about to begin. It would be one that explores what happens when, in the face of any circumstance, whether joyful or painful, we choose to have faith in generosity, kindness, and clear seeing. It would be the story of learning to have faith in our own innate goodness and capacity to love. It would be the story of seeing past the apparent randomness of 'sheer happenings' to uncover layers and layers of connection. It would be the story of knowing, even in the midst of great suffering, that we can still belong to life, that we're not cast out and alone." (2002, pp. 22–23).

Werner and Smith also found that "For the majority of the men and women in this cohort, faith was not tied to a specific formal religious affiliation but rather to confidence in some center of value…. [T]he resilient used their faith to maintain a positive vision of a meaningful life and to negotiate successfully an abundance of emotionally hazardous experiences" (1992, p. 207). This finding is perhaps best articulated by Mervlyn Kitashima, one of the "high-risk" children in Werner and Smith's study: "When there was no Grandma Kahaunaele, when there was no Ron Marsh, when there was no Wynona Reuben, [or] the many others — was that somewhere, someplace down the line, somebody had taught me, 'There is somebody greater than us who loves you.' And that was my hope and my belief. Whatever that translates for you — a belief in a God, a belief in a religion, a goal, a dream, something that we can all hang on to" (1997, p. 36).

The human search for meaning has often been labeled "spirituality," and as such has over the past decade been increasingly explored by the positive psychology movement and in health research. Researchers Pargament and Mahoney describe spirituality as finding "ways to understand and deal with our fundamental human insufficiency, the fact that there are limits to our control" (2002, p. 655).

The making of meaning is not just about transforming pain and suffering, but applies as well to living a rewarding life. In ongoing studies of what people seek in their everyday lives, Emmons and his colleagues (1998) categorize these needs as "strivings," such as achievement, intimacy, power, and spirituality. Spirituality was more highly correlated with measures of well-being than any other "striving." Baumeister (1991) identifies four meaning-related human needs: to have purpose, to have value, to feel a sense of efficacy, and to feel a sense of self-worth. Muller (1996) translates these needs into "four simple questions that reveal the beauty and meaning of [all] our lives": Who am I? What do I love? How shall I live? and How can I make a difference?

Meaning-making in the form of writing or speaking one's story is consistently associated in the research with positive health outcomes (Baumeister & Vohs, 2002; Esterling et al., 1999; Rubin, 1996) and even with academic ones (Pennebaker et al., 1990). According to Baumeister and his colleagues, the human organism is continually seeking stability in the face of change. "It turns to meaning to help create that stability. Thus, meaning can be regarded as one of humanity's tools for imposing stability on life" (Baumeister & Vohs, 2002, p. 609). In these terms, the search for meaning can be viewed as one of the "self-righting tendencies" tracked by Werner and Smith in their lifespan research.

The human organism is continually seeking stability in the face of change. It turns to meaning to help create that stability.

CHAPTER 3

A Perspective on Strengths

Before we look at just *how* children and youth develop personal resilience strengths, the developmental possibilities inherent in *all* young people, I want to provide a brief, four-point perspective on strengths that also serves as an interface to the chapters on environmental supports that follow.

A LANGUAGE OF STRENGTHS

First, because resilience and other strengths-based approaches hold that personal strengths result when people in family, school, and community settings create opportunities for youth to develop these strengths and capacities, we must have a *language* of strengths.

Having a language of strengths helps practitioners and parents begin to look for and find strengths in their young people and then to name and reflect back to youth the strengths they have witnessed. This is a critical component of strengths-based practice (Saleebey, 2001), which we will come back to in our discussion of environmental protective factors. This positive language helps teachers, parents, and other caregivers start to *reframe* how they see their young people, to begin their shift from seeing only risk to also seeing the incredible resilience of young people, especially those facing a whole range of challenges and adversity.

The previous chapter presented dozens of terms used for sometimes overlapping categories and sometimes hard-to-distinguish attributes. Even though the current language is not always definitive, the strengths exist and are being referred to in the terms reported. Researchers and practitioners must have a language for the human qualities that far too often remain invisible, unrecognized, unnamed, and unacknowledged.

In terms of the research community, having a nomenclature helps legitimate the study of strengths. The positive psychology movement, with leadership from the University of Pennsylvania, has undertaken a massive project, the *Values in Action (VIA) Classification of Strengths* (http://www.positivepsychology .org/taxonomy.htm), which is intended to be psychology's positive response to psychiatry's *Diagnostic and Statistical Manual (DSM).* With tongue only partly in cheek, Peterson and Seligman refer to the VIA document as a "manual of the sanities" (Peterson & Seligman, 2003, p. 4).

They hope the VIA taxonomy will legitimate and facilitate the study of character and that it will also promote the "cultivation" of character. In service of such, a language of human strengths enables researchers to empirically measure developmental outcomes from prevention and education interventions, and to better understand what works and what does not (Peterson & Seligman, 2003, p. 4).

THE DYNAMIC QUALITY OF STRENGTHS

Second is the importance of re-emphasizing that these strengths are *not* fixed personality traits. What a resilience perspective acknowledges is the dynamic, adaptational quality of resilience strengths, recognizing that they are not fixed personality characteristics that one either has or does not have, or even that the more one has the better. In fact, resilience theory, viewing resilience not as a fixed trait but as a dynamic and contextual process, recognizes that these internal "assets" can also be deficits if they are out of balance. For example, too much caring without the balance of autonomy can result in being "co-dependent." Too much autonomy without the balance of caring and connection can result in being self-centered and greedy.

Werner and Smith and others refer to healthy development as resulting in an "androgynous model of competence that includes being as well as doing, nurturance as well as risk-taking, for both sons and daughters" (1982, p. 162). Werner and Smith found that their resilient girls and women not only had high levels of social competence, a strength associated with being female, but also had high levels of autonomy and problem solving, strengths usually found in greater degree in males (1982, 1992). In contrast, their resilient boys and men not only had high levels of autonomy and problem solving, they also had high levels of social competence and relational skills. Similarly, these strengths vary in importance from culture to culture. For example, in cultures described as "individualist," (such as mainstream U.S. culture), autonomy is a highly valued personal strength, whereas "collectivist" cultures (such as many minority and immigrant cultures) place more value on social competence and connectedness skills and attitudes (Greenfield & Cocking, 1994).

Positive language helps teachers, parents, and other caregivers start to reframe how they see their young people, to begin their shift from seeing only risk to also seeing the incredible resilience of young people.

THE ROLE OF PSYCHOLOGICAL NEEDS AND INTRINSIC MOTIVATION

What appears to be driving the process of human development, resilience, and adaptation is an internal force, an amazing developmental wisdom often referred to as intrinsic motivation.

A third point reiterates the earlier discussion that, contrary to a common misunderstanding, these strengths are not special qualities that cause resilience. While the study of human strengths is a relatively recent phenomenon in psychology, research suggests instead that human beings are biologically prepared to develop these strengths and to use them for survival (Watson & Ecken, 2003). Because resilience strengths are available to all of us, Higgins asks that we "consider the resilient not as a unique subspecies but as fellow travelers, amplifying qualities, dynamics, and potentials inherent in us all" (1994, p. 66).

What appears to be driving this process of human development, resilience, and adaptation is an internal force, an amazing developmental wisdom often referred to as intrinsic motivation. Human beings are intrinsically motivated to meet basic psychological needs, including needs for belonging and affiliation, a sense of competence, feelings of autonomy, safety, and meaning. (Baumeister & Leary, 1995; Deci, 1995; Hillman, 1996; Maslow, 1954; Richardson, 2002; Ryan & Deci, 2000; Sandler, 2000).

Because of our psychological need for belonging, we seek to relate to and connect with others, and thus develop our social competence strengths. Psychologists refer to this drive as our affiliation/belongingness adaptional system (Baumeister & Leary, 1995). Our psychological need to feel competent drives us to develop our cognitive problem-solving skills (Pearce, 1977/1992). This need to feel competent, combined with the psychological need to feel autonomous, leads us to seek people and opportunities that allow us to experience a sense of our own power and accomplishment. Psychologists refer to this as our mastery motivational system (Bandura, 1997). Our safety motivational system includes the need to avoid pain and maintain physical survival — which drives us to develop not only problem solving but also social competence, autonomy, and even purpose. Our need to find meaning in our lives motivates us to seek people, places, and transformational experiences that make us feel we have a sense of purpose, future, and inter-connectedness with life (Csikszentmihalyi, 1990; Hillman, 1996).

How these needs are expressed and met varies, of course, not only within a person and over time but from person to person and from culture to culture. The bottom line belief for resilience and youth development theory and practice is that these psychological needs are a given. These needs are referred to by developmental psychologists as "fundamental protective human adaptational systems" (Masten & Reed, 2002, p. 82). All human beings are compelled to meet these needs throughout the lifespan. For young people, whether these needs are allowed expression in positive, prosocial ways depends to a great extent on the people, places, and experiences they encounter in their families, schools, and communities.

THE ROLE OF ENVIRONMENT

A fourth and last point in looking at resilience strengths is to understand that because these strengths are dynamic, contextual, and culturally expressed, and arise from our intrinsic motivation to meet basic psychological needs, they are not learned, for the most part or in a lasting way, through a social skills program or a life skills curriculum that attempts to directly teach them. A long history of prevention program evaluation (Kohn, 1997; Kreft & Brown, 1998) testifies to the short-lived effects of eight-week life skills programs. That this approach still predominates in both education and prevention speaks to the strong hold that behaviorism — in terms of focusing on concrete behavior change — and "kid-fixing" have over our culture and institutions.

From a developmental (as opposed to behavioral) perspective, resilience strengths are critical survival skills, intrinsically motivated or biologically driven, and culturally expressed — an apparently fail-safe adaptational system: Survival needs drive healthy development. Healthy development results in survival.

The catch, of course, is providing for these needs to be expressed in healthy, culturally valued, and prosocial ways. Were we to work with children and youth from a developmental perspective, we would understand that the deeper issue when a child doesn't express these critical skills — let's say for empathy — is not that the child has no drive to be empathic, it's that in the child's environment, expression of empathy is not valued and models of empathy are absent. If we truly want youth to develop their propensity to behave with empathy, then we must have people who model empathy and who create a climate in which empathy is the norm. If we want youth to have good problem-solving and decision-making skills, then we must provide them with the opportunities to actively engage in problem solving and to make real and valued decisions about things they care about. Alfie Kohn explains this process as follows: "It is widely understood that people

"It is widely understood that people learn by example. But adults who are respectful of children are not just modeling a skill or behavior, they are meeting the emotional needs of those children, thereby helping to create the psychological conditions for children to treat others respectfully."

— Alfie Kohn

Positive youth development depends on the quality of the environment — the available supports, messages, and opportunities young people find in the people, places, and experiences in their lives.

learn by example. But adults who are respectful of children are not just modeling a skill or behavior, they are meeting the emotional needs of those children, thereby helping to create the psychological conditions for children to treat others respectfully" (Kohn, 1997, p. 15; Watson & Ecken, 2003).

In summary, resilience research continues to validate the model of human development identified over a decade ago in *Fostering Resiliency in Kids* — "a transactional-ecological model…in which the human personality is viewed as a self-righting mechanism that is engaged in active, ongoing adaptation to its environment" (Benard, 1991, p. 2; Bronfenbrenner, 1974; Pianta & Walsh, 1998; Werner & Smith, 2001). Developing and enhancing the resiliency strengths that can be engendered because of this "self-righting mechanism" are the natural tasks of youth development (Gibbs, 2001; Masten & Coatsworth, 1998; Sandler, 2001).

As research continues to shed light on this process, it continues to situate positive youth development in the context of family, school, and community — recognizing that "Human development is a cultural process; … that people develop as participants in cultural communities" (Rogoff, 2003, p. 39). Young people learn what is lived around them, for the most part through modeling, cultural practices, and direct experience. Positive youth development, then, depends on the *quality of the environment* — the available supports, messages, and opportunities young people find in the people, places, and experiences in their lives. This is the focus of our next chapters.

environmental protective factors

CHAPTER 4
Environmental Protective Factors

How do so many young people facing even extreme challenges manage to tap their innate potential for healthy growth and development, for transformation and change? Who or what helps them grow up — in the often-quoted words of resilience literature — to "love well, work well, play well, and expect well"? (Garmezy, 1974; Werner & Smith, 1982). As Werner and Smith report, "The life stories of the resilient youngsters now grown into adulthood teach us that competence, confidence, and caring can flourish, even under adverse circumstances, if children encounter persons who provide them with the secure basis for the development of trust, autonomy, and initiative. From odds successfully overcome springs hope — a gift each of us can share with a child — at home, in the classroom, on the playground, or in the neighborhood" (1992, p. 209).

As the preceding section on personal strengths makes clear, the preponderance of resilience-related research identifies resilience as a universal, developmental capacity of every human being. What this innate developmental capacity requires to produce good developmental outcomes is a nurturing environment in which young people can meet their inborn, psychological needs for belonging and affiliation, a sense of competence, feelings of autonomy, and safety — all of which contribute to a personal sense of hope. Leading resilience researchers now tie adversity and risk directly to factors that interfere with young people's abilities to satisfy these needs (Masten & Reed, 2002; Sandler, 2001) and recognize that there are specific environmental factors that protect youth from risk. According to Masten and Reed, "The findings on resilience suggest that the greatest threats to children are those adversities that undermine the basic human protective systems for development" (2002, p. 83).

No matter whose conceptualizations we look at, these protective factors or systems outline a very simple recipe — albeit not an easy one — of *caring relationships, high expectation messages,* and *opportunities for participation and contribution* (see Figure 3). These three "environmental protective factors," first conceptualized in *Fostering Resiliency in Kids: Protective Factors in the Family, School, and Community* (Benard, 1991), have not only held up under scrutiny of research, but have formed the guiding principles of many prevention and education efforts over the last decade and more. They map well to the Search

Institute's categories of "external assets" and basically describe what the youth development field refers to as "supports and opportunities." They are also commonly referred to as "social capital," the interpersonal resources necessary for healthy development and life success.

Figure 3. Protective Factors in Young People's Environments

		YOUTH ENVIRONMENTS		
		Families	Schools	Communities
PROTECTIVE FACTORS	Caring Relationships	✓	✓	✓
	High Expectations	✓	✓	✓
	Opportunities to Participate & Contribute	✓	✓	✓

Keep in mind that while these environmental protective factors are introduced below and discussed in later chapters as if each were a separate entity, they are instead aspects or components of a dynamic protective *process*, in which they must work together. For example, caring relationships without high expectations or opportunities for meaningful participation foster dependency and co-dependency — not positive youth development. High expectations without caring relationships and support to help youth meet them are a cruel "shape-up or ship-out" approach associated with negative outcomes. And, one more example, caring relationships with high expectation messages but no opportunities for a child's active participation and contribution create a frustrating situation that blocks the natural process of youth development.

CARING RELATIONSHIPS

The term "caring relationships" conveys loving support — the message of being there for a youth, of trust, and of unconditional love. Resilient survivors describe relationships characterized by "quiet availability," "fundamental positive regard," and "simple sustained kindness" — a touch on the shoulder, a smile, a greeting (Higgins, 1994, pp. 324–25). Adults who have overcome childhoods of abuse "strongly recommended that those of you who touch the life of a child constructively, even briefly, should *never* underestimate your possible corrective impact on that child" (p. 325). Likewise, straightforward respect, having a person "acknowledge us, see us for who we are — as their equal in value and importance" figures high in turnaround relationships (Meier, 1995, p. 120).

In particular, caring relationships are characterized by a sense of compassion — nonjudgmental love that looks beneath negative behaviors in search of their causes. Compassionate caregivers do not take a young person's behavior personally. They understand that no matter how negative it may be, it is the best that youth can muster given how she or he *sees* the world.

Finally, caregivers who are interested in, actively listen to, and get to know the gifts of their young people convey the message, "You are important in this world; you matter." In Alice Miller's account of resilient survivors of childhood sexual abuse and trauma, being able to tell their story to someone who believed them was both validating and healing: "It turns out in every case [of successful adaptation] that a sympathetic and helpful witness confirmed the child's perceptions, thus making it possible for him to recognize that he had been wronged" (1990, p. 50–51).

According to a report from the National Research Council and the Institute of Medicine, "Supportive relationships are critical 'mediums' of development. They provide an environment of reinforcement, good modeling, and constructive feedback for physical, intellectual, psychological, and social growth." Furthermore, the report continues, "The attentive, caring, and wise voice of a supportive adult gets internalized and becomes part of the youth's own voice" (Eccles & Gootman, 2002, p. 96).

HIGH EXPECTATIONS

At the heart of caring relationships are high expectations, defined as clear, positive, and youth-centered expectations. "Clear" expectations refers to the guidance and regulatory function that caregivers must provide developing young people. This means creating a sense of structure and safety through rules and disciplinary approaches that are not only perceived as fair by young people but that include youth in their creation.

"Positive" and "youth-centered" messages are those that communicate the adult's deep belief in the young person's innate resilience and self-righting capacities and that challenge the youth to become all he or she can be. "She believed in me when I didn't believe in myself" is a refrain echoed by many adults in the author's workshops as they reflect on transformative messages in their lives. An often-ignored subtlety of this common sentiment is that the adult's high expectations were based on the strengths, interests, hopes, and dreams of the youth — not on what the adult wanted the youth to do or be.

> Caring relationships are characterized by "fundamentally positive regard" and "simple, sustained kindness."

Turnaround people help

youth see the power

they have.

When caregivers are youth-centered, using the young person's own strengths, interests, goals, and dreams as the beginning point for learning and helping, they tap young people's intrinsic motivation, their existing, innate drive for learning and personal growth. For example, John Seita, who grew up in multiple foster homes, tells the story of his turnaround social worker: "Mr. Lambert, who was a recent graduate of college when he first met me, had no training in bonding with relationship-resistant youth. Few of us do. But he reached me through the back door. He doggedly attempted to find a special interest of mine, namely my dreams of being a sports hero. Although I did not trust other adults, he connected with me through a special interest" (Seita et al., 1996, p. 88).

Turnaround people assist youth, especially those who have been labeled or oppressed, in understanding their innate resilience, their personal power to reframe their life narratives from damaged victim to resilient survivor (Wolin & Wolin, 1993). Turnaround people help youth see the power they have to think differently about and construct alternative stories of their lives. As Seligman and his colleagues (1995) present this shift in perspective, turnaround people help youth (1) not to take *personally* the adversity in their lives ("You are not the cause of, nor can you control, your father's drinking"); (2) not to see adversity as *permanent* ("This too shall pass"); and (3) not to see setbacks as *pervasive* ("This is only one part of your life experience").

In the resiliency model presented here, high expectations serve as an *inter*-personal factor through which young people internalize high expectations for themselves, thus transforming them into an *intra*-personal attribute. "When the message one consistently hears — from family members, from teachers, from significant others in one's environment — is, 'You are a bright and capable person,' one naturally sees oneself as a bright and capable person, a person with that resilient trait, a sense of purpose and bright future" (Benard, 1991, p. 12).

OPPORTUNITIES FOR PARTICIPATION AND CONTRIBUTION

Creating the opportunities for youth participation and contribution is a natural outgrowth of relationships based on caring and high expectations. Providing youth the chance to participate in engaging, challenging, and interesting activities, or "flow" experiences, promotes the whole range of personal resilience strengths (Hattie et al., 1997; Larson, 2000; Werner & Smith, 1992). According to Larson's research on initiative, "the conditions that make structured youth activities a fertile context for the development of initiative … also make them a rich context for the development of an array of other positive qualities, from altruism to identity" (2000, p. 178). Certainly, for youth to develop their personal resilience strengths related to a special interest, creativity, and imagination, they need to have real opportunities to do so.

Opportunities for participation in group or cooperative activities can help young people fulfill their strong psychological needs for belonging. Werner and Smith found that activities that allowed youth "to be a part of a cooperative enterprise, such as being a cheerleader for the home team or raising an animal for the 4-H Club" connected them to a group that could, if needed, serve them as a surrogate family (1992, p. 205).

Another important kind of participation involves having opportunities for reflection and dialog around issues meaningful to youth — for adolescents, these especially relate to sexuality, drug use, and family communication. Young people continually identify a need to give voice to their realities, with their families, in school, and in their communities — especially in a small group context (Brown & D'Emidio-Caston, 1995). When caregivers provide youth with the opportunity to discuss their experiences, beliefs, attitudes, and feelings — and encourage them to critically question societal messages, whether from the media or their own conditioned thinking around these issues, caregivers empower youth to be critical thinkers and decision-makers around the important issues in their own lives.

Opportunities for creative expression through all forms of the arts — writing, storytelling, and the performing and visual arts — are a vital component in youth participation. By providing youth with ways to use their creativity and imagination, caregivers help them develop transformative resilience strengths.

Opportunities for participation also include having chances to problem-solve and make decisions. When caregivers are able to identify and provide appropriate opportunities for freedom and self-determination, they help young people develop autonomy and self-control. Authentic decision-making and leadership responsibilities are often the characteristics distinguishing successful from unsuccessful youth programs and settings (Gambone & Arbreton, 1997; McLaughlin et al., 1994; Tierney et al., 1995; Werner & Smith, 1992).

When opportunities for participation incorporate opportunities for contribution, and youth are able to "give back" their gifts to their families, schools, and communities, they no longer see themselves as simply recipients of what adults have to offer — even if it is the good stuff of caring and positive beliefs — but as active contributors to the settings in which they live. Giving back

Authentic decision-making and leadership responsibilities are often the characteristics distinguishing successful from unsuccessful youth programs and settings.

is a powerful "hook" for all youth, especially for those not used to thinking of themselves as successful. It helps them reframe their self-perceptions from being a problem and *receiver* of services to being a resource and *provider* of services.

In all these ways — through having the opportunities to be heard, to voice one's opinion, to make choices, to have responsibilities, to engage in active problem solving, to express one's imagination, to work with and help others, and to give one's gift back to the community — youth develop the attitudes and competencies characteristic of healthy development and successful learning, the personal strengths associated with social competence, problem solving, a positive sense of self, and a positive sense of the future.

In sum, even when we look beyond the longitudinal studies of human development, which anchor much resilience research, and examine the research on the characteristics of healthy families, schools, neighborhood-based organizations, and workplace organizations — and even include what we've learned from motivational psychology — we see the power of these three protective factors to promote positive development and successful outcomes (see Figure 4). Successful development in any human system is dependent on the quality of the relationships, beliefs, and opportunities for participation in that system.

The chapters that follow highlight how these protective factors have played out in some of the key research and practice of the last decade, specifically in terms of young people's families, schools, and communities. It has been a decade of abundance in research support for resilience and youth development, and the summaries below make no attempt to be exhaustive.

Figure 4. The Role of Protective Factors in Human Systems

Protective Factors	facilitate →	Positive Development	leading to →	Successful Outcomes
Caring Relationships		Brain Development		Successful Individuals
High Expectations		Human Development		Healthy Families
Participation		System Change		Effective Schools
				Healthy Communities
				Learning Organizations

Positive development and successful outcomes in any human system depend on the quality of the relationships, beliefs, and opportunities for participation.

CHAPTER 5
Family Protective Factors

Do parents matter? This was the critical question addressed by family research in the past decade. Psychologist Judith Harris's (1998) controversial book, *The Nurture Assumption: Why Children Turn Out the Way They Do,* made the case that parents, especially as traditionally defined, have a more limited effect on a young person's development than is commonly believed in our culture. Similarly, Stephanie Coontz's (1992) earlier historical account of family life, *The Way We Never Were: American Families and the Nostalgia Trap*, challenged the idea that the nuclear family, a very recent organization in terms of human history, is the only and "best" structure for rearing our children.

While armies of researchers and advocates have lined up on both sides of this values-laden controversy, much of the research cited in both books (several hundred studies) supports the findings of resilience research — in other words that, yes, the family and parenting do matter, but, no, they are not the only nor even always the most potent influence (Barber & Olsen, 1997) on young people. A child grows up in many settings beyond the home — preschools, schools, community-based organizations, youth groups, and friendship groups, which can also play a powerful role in their healthy and successful development. If this were *not* the case, we would not see resilient survivors of abusive, drug-using, mentally ill, or absent families nor would we see healthy adults who grew up in nontraditional families — divorced, gay/lesbian, single-parent, or foster families.

Much of this controversy, especially as it has focused on single-parenting, can be resolved by closely examining the numbers and percentages of children who actually experience adverse outcomes (psychological, behavioral, social, and academic) as a result of living in a single-parent home. For example, a recent rigorous study comparing Swedish children in single-parent and two-parent households did indeed find the former at roughly twice the risk to develop a psychiatric illness, to attempt or commit suicide, and to develop an alcohol-related disorder (Weitoft et al., 2003). This study was highly publicized, with newspaper headlines such as "One Parent, Twice the Trouble (Ross, 2003). However, what was not addressed by either the

The effect of parents as a protective factor for children is most dramatic in extreme conditions.

researchers or the reporters were the actual percentages of youth with adverse outcomes. In fact, only 2 percent of the girls and 1.5 percent of the boys from single-parent families developed psychiatric problems as children and adolescents. As young adults, the rates dropped to 0.9 percent and 0.7 percent. The untold story is that 98 percent of children and adolescents in single-parent families did *not* have psychiatric disorders. Similarly, 98 percent of the girls and 99 percent of the boys did *not* commit suicide; 99 percent of the girls and 98.8 percent of the boys did *not* commit a violent act; 99 percent of the girls and 98.8 percent of the boys did *not* develop an alcohol-related disorder, and so on (Weitoft et al., 2003).

HOW IMPORTANT ARE PARENTS?

Even while acknowledging that children can succeed regardless of their families, findings from the National Longitudinal Study of Adolescent Health (Add Health) point to the importance of the parent. This study surveyed 90,000 middle and high school students and interviewed a 20,000-student sample plus their parents. Blum and other Add Health researchers Beuhring and Rinehart (2000) conclude that commonly regarded "predictors" of adolescent behavior — race/ethnicity, family income, and family structure — turn out to be relatively weak (and "not especially amenable to change"). Instead, in a more fine-grained analysis of the data, Blum, Shew, Beuhring, and others (2000) report, "The one most consistently protective factor found was the presence of a positive parent-family relationship."

The effect of parents as a protective factor for children is most dramatic in extreme conditions — for children growing up in dangerous or resource-poor communities or in the midst of war — when the family often is a child's only reliable resource (Garbarino et al., 1992; Richters & Martinez, 1993). In their studies of resilience in violent communities, Richters and Martinez found that "The odds of early adaptational failure among children from stable and safe homes were only about 6 percent; these increased by more than 300 percent for children from homes rated as either unstable or unsafe, and by more than 1,500 percent for children from homes rated as both unstable and unsafe" (1993, p. 625).

Because divorce is a factor in so many families, and usually contributes at least initially to family instability, the research represented in E. Mavis Hetherington's three-decade-long study of almost 1,400 families and more than 2,500 children is another important lens for viewing the role of parents and families in children's development. Her study, published as *For Better or For Worse: Divorce Reconsidered* (Hetherington & Kelly, 2002), which included a control group of intact families, documented that 75 to 80 percent of children from divorced homes are "coping reasonably well and functioning in the normal range" and "go on to have reasonably happy or sometimes very happy lives." Given that Hetherington's research methods are regarded by her peers as the "gold standard" (K. Peterson, 2002), her study convincingly refutes less rigorous but widely reported research indicating less positive outcomes for children from divorced families (Blakeslee & Wallerstein, 1989; Wallerstein et al., 2000).

Teenage single mothers have also been surprisingly successful, in terms both of their children's well-being and their own. Furstenberg and his colleagues (1998) studied 500 teenage mothers and their children in an urban environment. They found that most of the children were doing well, and so were their mothers. Furthermore, they found that the children's successful adolescent development was directly related to the economic and social support services provided to teen mothers. Werner and Smith's 26-year follow-up analysis of the teen mothers in their cohort found parallel outcomes, with 92 percent of the teenage mothers staging a "remarkable metamorphosis" by midlife (2001, p. 93).

The common-sense, good news from all this research, if policymakers, politicians, and advocates can distance themselves from the rhetoric, is that the critical issues in supporting children's healthy development have been identified. If we truly want to improve the lives of children, first, our society must support all family caregivers, regardless of family structure. As Coontz states, "Both contemporary studies and historical experience show that children are resilient enough to adapt to many different innovations in family patterns: When they cannot adapt, this is caused more often by the economic and social context in which those innovations take place than by their parents' 'wrong turns' away from traditional family patterns" (1992, p. 206).

Second, we must support those outside of families who serve as children's caregivers. As documented by Werner and Smith (1992), the most powerful protective factor in the life histories of resilient children was the presence of one caring adult in the child's life, most powerfully a parent, but often a mentor or surrogate parent.

Third, because families do not and cannot provide all the support that young people need, the other settings in which children grow up — schools and communities — must recognize as their primary role the healthy

> **"Both contemporary studies and historical experience show that children are resilient enough to adapt to many different innovations in family patterns."**
>
> **— Stephanie Coontz**

physical, social, emotional, and cognitive development of young people. The fundamental and comprehensive aspects of this role are not always appreciated. Schools and communities are powerful and even transformative developmental influences in the lives of children, especially when they are called on to compensate for challenges in the family setting (Barber & Olsen, 1997; Masten & Coatsworth, 1998; Werner & Smith, 1992).

For some parents, understanding the help that others provide in their children's development — or the limits of their own influence — can help them to relax and tap into their common sense in parenting. As Harris points out, "The nurture assumption [the idea that parents are totally responsible for how their children turn out] has turned children into objects of anxiety. Parents are nervous about doing the wrong thing, fearful that a stray word or glance might ruin their child's chances forever" (1998, p. 352). In contrast, Furstenberg found that when parents felt a sense of self-efficacy or "beliefs of mastery as a parent," their adolescents did better in school and were able to avoid social- and health-risk behaviors (Furstenberg et al., 1998, p. 121).

THE ROLE OF PARENTING STYLE

Research into the qualities that differentiate effective and ineffective parenting has burgeoned along with a general interest beginning in the 1980s into the *qualities* of all the contexts that contribute to healthy adolescent development. In terms of protective factors, "Parenting style rather than family structure has been found to be the main determinant of effective family functioning and adolescent well-being" (McFarlane et al., 1995), including school success (Steinberg, 1997). In terms of risk factors, parental conflict (parent-to-parent) continued to be identified as the major family risk factor and source of stress for adolescents (Henricson & Roker, 2000).

Most of the research on parenting has continued to validate the three-pronged approach advocated a decade ago in *Fostering Resiliency in Kids* (Benard, 1991) and reiterated in this volume: caring relationships, high and *youth-centered* expectations, and opportunities for participation and contribution. In fact, an impressive body of research on the role of the family in adolescent development and school success has flowed over the last 10 years from a team of researchers at Stanford University, the University of Wisconsin, and the University of Pennsylvania. They have identified three key qualities of the parent-child relationship — warmth/connection, guidance/regulation, and psychological autonomy-granting (Steinberg, 2000) — which map well to our three protective factors (caring relationships, high expectations, and opportunities for participation and contribution). Similarly, other bodies of research, including the Seattle Social Development Project (Hill et al., 1999), the Rochester Youth Development Study (Thornberry, 1998), and the Pittsburgh Youth Study (Lahey et al., 1999) have all found adverse adolescent outcomes associated with the lack of a caring parent-adolescent relationship and poor parental regulation or family management practices.

"Authoritative" is the term Laurence Steinberg and his colleagues use (building on the pioneering research of Diana Baumrind) to describe a parent who is "warm and involved, but is firm and consistent in establishing and enforcing guidelines, limits, and developmentally appropriate expectations" and "encourages and permits the adolescent to develop his or her own opinions and beliefs" (Steinberg, 2000, p. 173). As Steinberg continues in this important review article, "Each component of authoritativeness — warmth, firmness, and psychological autonomy-granting — makes an independent contribution to healthy adolescent development, in overlapping, although slightly different ways.... Perhaps the most important conclusion to emerge from our work is that adolescents raised in authoritative homes continue to show the same sorts of advantages in psychosocial development and mental health over their non-authoritatively raised peers that were apparent in studies of younger children" (p. 173). In another study, Masten and her colleagues (1999) followed over 200 children for 10 years and found that parenting quality, measured as a combination of "warmth, expectations, and structure," was a major protective factor sustaining healthy development in the face of adversities such as poverty and personal traumas, from both the parents' and teens' perspectives.

In terms of cultural differences in parenting style, Steinberg's review of the literature holds that "Minority youngsters raised in authoritative homes fare better than their peers from non-authoritative homes with respect to psychosocial development, symptoms of internalized distress, and problem behavior" (2000, p. 175). Several researchers have challenged the efficacy of authoritativeness with African American and Asian American youth, proposing that a more structured, "authoritarian" parenting style, which features higher levels of behavioral and psychological control, is more protective (Baldwin et al., 1993; Chao, 1994, 2001; Walker-Barnes & Mason, 2001). Interestingly, Ruth Chao (2001) found positive effects of authoritative parenting for second-generation Chinese Americans but not for first-generation Chinese. Perhaps some of these discrepant findings can be explained as Chao (1999) and others (Walker-Barnes & Mason, 2001) have by the fact that parental emphasis on obedience and respect have different

"Each component of authoritativeness — warmth, firmness, and psychological autonomy-granting — makes an independent contribution to healthy adolescent development, in overlapping, although slightly different ways."

— Laurence Steinberg

meanings in Asian and African American cultures than in American culture generally. In African American and Asian cultures, parents see an emphasis on obedience and respect more often as an attribute of caring and "relationship closeness" than as an attribute of control.

In Steinberg's review, the one area in which authoritative vs. authoritarian parenting style outcomes are ambiguous for African American and Asian American youth is that of school performance. On the other hand, Furstenberg and his colleagues' (1998) longitudinal study of primarily African American Philadelphia neighborhoods associates an authoritative pattern of parenting with better academic outcomes. (The effects of cultural differences are also at issue in our later discussion, pages 57–61, of autonomy and opportunities to participate and contribute.)

Apparently, so long as adolescents feel "connected" to their families (operationalized as feeling close to parents, feeling satisfied with family relationships, and feeling loved and cared for), the Add Health researchers found this "connected" relationship was protective against every adolescent health-risk behavior from alcohol, tobacco, and other drug use to emotional distress, violence, and risky sexual behavior (Resnick et al., 1997). Likewise, the California Department of Education's Healthy Kids Resilience & Youth Development Module, which is based on the resilience framework developed by Benard (1991) and presented here, has found similar relationships between family protective factors and the risk behaviors so far examined: binge drinking, tobacco smoking, marijuana use at school, and bringing a weapon to school (Benard, 2002). The greater the levels of caring relationships, high expectation beliefs, and meaningful participation in the family, the less young people are involved in these health-risk behaviors.

CARING RELATIONSHIPS IN FAMILIES

What describes a caring parent? Words like emotionally supportive and responsive, nurturing, warm, empathic, accepting, and unconditional are common in the literature. "Unfailingly loving" would apply to Lauren Slater's foster mother. As Sylvia Rockwell describes Lauren's situation, "This young woman was hospitalized repeatedly for suicide attempts as a teenager. At the age of 14 she was given over as a ward of the state by a mother who had abused her and no longer wanted her. However, she credits the four years she spent in foster care with an unfailingly loving foster mother for her eventual decision to give herself a chance at health and happiness" (1998, p. 16).

Rak's case studies (2002) of "heros in the nursery" document the findings of earlier resilience research (Anthony, 1974; Rutter et al., 1979; Werner & Smith, 1982) in terms of the power of one caregiver early in the child's life who "provided a good-enough nurturing and bonding experience" (Rak, 2002, p. 258). In the Mother-Child Project, a longitudinal study of high-risk children and families, researchers found that the major protective factor for children growing up in poverty and its attendant lack of resources was the "emotionally responsive caregiving" available in the family (Egeland et al., 1993). As Add Health researchers have reported, family "connectedness," consisting of "feelings of warmth, love, and caring from parents" (Resnick et al., 1997, p. 830) was equally protective whether the parent was custodial or noncustodial; the critical issue was that the adolescent felt listened to, paid attention to, and special.

Steinberg and his colleagues found that parental warmth is "a general facilitator of mental health, academic competence, and overall psychological functioning" (2000, p. 173). Barber and Olsen (1997) found a direct association between warmth and care in the family and adolescent social competence. "Consistent, stable, positive, emotional connections with significant others, like parents, appear to equip children with important social skills as well as a sense that the world is safe, secure, and predictable" (Barber, 1997, p. 8). Henry and others (1996) found that parental encouragement, warmth, and praise were associated with adolescents' higher levels of empathy and caring for others. Herman and her colleagues (1997) found a direct positive relationship between teens who experienced caring relationships in their families and their academic achievement.

Parental empathy is a primary first step in developing a caring relationship, according to Brooks and Goldstein (2001) in *Raising Resilient Children*. Empathy, they point out, helps parents accept their children for who they are and provides them with the unconditional acceptance that children need in order to develop a basic sense of trust. Fortunately, according to the theory proposed by Thomas Lewis and his colleagues in *A General Theory of Love* (2001), empathy is a built-in biological capacity of the limbic system — "a sensory system inside the brain designed to [provide] information about the emotional state inside someone else's brain" (Ellis, 2001, p. 50). As identified in research about the Health Realization approach to parenting (Mills, 1995), one of the most effective ways to help parents love and care for their children is to teach them to relax enough to allow this natural empathic process to occur.

Parental empathy is a primary first step in developing a caring relationship.

HIGH EXPECTATIONS IN FAMILIES

High expectations in families can provide the guidance that contributes to a young person's safety, can communicate an attitude of believing in the child's worth and competence, and can be the catalyst for helping a young person to find her or his strengths.

In our typology, the regulatory function of parenting — providing clear expectations in the form of guidance and structure for behavior — meets children's and adolescents' needs for safety. This function goes by many terms in the literature: parental regulation, parental monitoring, family management, and supervision, to name a few. Steinberg and his colleagues found that a parenting style characterized by "firmness" in setting expectations was protective in promoting positive youth outcomes, especially by preventing antisocial behavior, such as drug and alcohol abuse and delinquency, but also in contributing to academic competence (Steinberg, 2000, p. 173).

Another component of high expectations is the positive belief on the part of parents that their children will be successful, that they have "what it takes." Higgins relates the importance of this quality in a quote from one of her "resilient adults": "I've always had the sense that by [my grandmother's] allowing me to watch how she did things and treating me as though she thought I could be like her, there was a message: 'You can do this. Somewhere in you is all the right stuff. You've just got to find it'" (1994, p. 336). According to Brooks and Goldstein, "When parents convey expectations in an accepting, loving, supportive manner, children are often motivated to exceed those expectations" (2001, p. 134).

High expectations on the part of parents and other family caregivers for their children's school success has remained a consistent predictor of positive health and academic outcomes for youth over the years, and increasingly so for children in minority families (Clark, 1984; Gandara, 1995; Herman et al., 1997; Kim & Chun, 1994). All of these studies identified parents who not only had high educational expectations for their children but also were willing to actively advocate for their children. The Add Health study (Resnick et al., 1997) found that high parental expectations for their child's school achievement were moderately protective against children's emotional distress.

Parental high expectation beliefs are not limited to academic success; they include encouraging children to find their strengths, their calling, their special interest and gift. Parents nurture these strengths by connecting children to programs, people, and places that will help them develop their calling. John Seita and his colleagues (1996) refer to this as "talent scouting." Brooks and Goldstein (2001) describe this aspect of raising resilient children as helping children find their "island of competence." Furstenberg and his colleagues (1998) found that the most successful African American parents in their longitudinal study were actively engaged in these "promoting" strategies that connected their children to outside resources and supports to further develop their interests and competencies.

Parental high

expectations include

helping children find

their "island

of competence."

Sometimes talent scouting requires good detective work, for many children's strengths are embedded in what may appear to be a deficit. Continual clowning around, for example, is often punished in families and schools. However, as we've seen, humor remains one of the most protective strengths a person can have in terms of physical and mental health. The challenge for parents and other caregivers is to find an appropriate channel for what can be annoying behavior so that this potential asset is not shamed out of existence. Many books over the last decade have focused on how to do this reframing with especially challenging children. *Raising Your Spirited Child* (Kurcinka, 1992) remains one of the best and most popular examples.

OPPORTUNITIES FOR PARTICIPATION AND CONTRIBUTION IN FAMILIES

In families, the protective factors of participation and contribution depend on parents being able to provide children with both responsibility and autonomy. The degree to which a child experiences either must be developmentally appropriate but also, researchers are finding, sensitive to conditions in the child's particular environment.

While being able to contribute by having valued responsibilities and roles within the family has not been a focus of research attention this last decade, historically it has been associated with positive developmental (including health) outcomes for youth (and adults) and good parenting (see Benard, 1991, for a summary). Janice Cohn's (1997) book, *Raising Compassionate, Courageous Children in a Violent World*, cites several studies documenting higher levels of well-being and life satisfaction for individuals who are involved in something beyond themselves. Similarly, Werner and Smith (1992) found that "acts of required helpfulness," such as caring for younger siblings or managing the household when a parent was incapacitated, were positively associated with overcoming a challenging childhood and with life success.

Young people's opportunities to participate in the family are often tied to parenting style, and especially to parents' granting of autonomy. Parents who create opportunities for their children and adolescents to have some decision-making power and to solve problems on their own help meet their children's basic need for psychological autonomy. Likewise parents who listen to their children as people deserving respect and attention grant them psychological autonomy. According to Steinberg, "Psychological autonomy-granting functions much like warmth as a general protective factor, but seems to have special benefits as a protection against anxiety, depression, and other forms of internalized distress" (2000, p. 174). Eccles et al. also found "positive associations between the extent of the adolescents' participation in family decision making and indicators of both intrinsic school motivation and positive self-esteem" (1993, p. 98). This fits nicely with the self-efficacy research discussed earlier since it is through autonomy experiences that individuals develop a sense of their own power and control, known moderators against anxiety and depression.

The gradual granting of autonomy experiences (or opportunities for participation) and the need to balance autonomy with guidance and control is perhaps the most challenging aspect of parenting, especially during the adolescent years when the biological need for autonomy asserts itself as a primary drive. As prominent adolescent researchers have written, "It is not easy for parents to determine the optimal level of autonomy versus control for their children at all ages. One would predict strained relationships wherever there is a poor fit between the child's desire for increasing autonomy and the opportunities for independence and autonomy provided by the child's parents" (Eccles et al., 1993, p. 97).

Parents whose efforts, however imperfect, are at least on the continuum of granting their children appropriate psychological (and behavioral) autonomy stand in sharp contrast to parents who wield psychological control. "Psychological control refers to parental behaviors that are intrusive and manipulative of children's thoughts, feelings, and attachments to parents" (Barber, 2002, p. 15). Psychological control appears to be a particularly destructive way *not* to grant psychological autonomy. This last decade has witnessed a burgeoning of interest, led by Brian Barber and his colleagues, in the concept of parental psychological control (Barber, 1996, 2002; Barber & Olsen, 1997). In characterizing parental psychological control as a violation of the child's psychological self, these researchers point to terms in the literature, including manipulative, constraining, guilt-inducing, love withdrawal, anxiety-instilling, possessive, dominant, and enmeshing, that refer to psychological control.

Contributors to *Intrusive Parenting: How Psychological Control Affects Children and Adolescents* (Barber, 2002) marshal convincing research that parental psychological control is associated with disturbances in psycho-emotional boundaries between the child and parent and, hence, with the development of an independent sense of self and identity. They report that besides these negative effects on children's self well-being processes (such resilience strengths as autonomy, identity, self-awareness, and self-efficacy), psychological control also increases children's internalized problems, such as depression, suicidal ideation, withdrawn behavior, eating disorders, and passive resistance. Similarly, they found a consistent positive relationship between psychological control and externalized problems (delinquency, substance abuse, aggression, defiance, and deviance) as well as with decreased academic achievement.

The research reported in *Intrusive Parenting* looks at parental control across cultures and, as Barber and Harmon report, "The findings are consistent in showing that perceived psychological control is associated positively and significantly to both forms of problem behavior [internalized and externalized] in all nine cultures [we've examined]. Particularly noteworthy is that these patterns hold in two collectivist cultures — India and Gaza — in which less emphasis is placed on individual autonomy than is in more individualistic cultures" (2002, p. 44).

Benard's thesis, as discussed earlier, is that while autonomy support may look different in different cultures and may vary in degree, autonomy is a basic human need and, thus, healthy development requires autonomy-supportive environments. The research reported by Barber leads him to make a similar assertion: "The effects of parental psychological control are as ubiquitous as they have recently been shown to be because this behavior intrudes on a basic human drive for some form of psychological and emotional autonomy, and that therefore, these negative effects should be found broadly across cultures" (2002, p. 44).

Referring back to our discussion of authoritarian and authoritative parenting, it should be pointed out that authoritarian parenting, while more controlling than authoritative parenting, is not synonymous with parental psychological control. Autonomy-granting can be problematic for parents living in dangerous and under-resourced communities, but restricting

Psychological control appears to be a particularly destructive way *not* to grant psychological autonomy.

Autonomy-granting can be problematic for parents living in dangerous and under-resourced communities.

children's autonomy need not be manipulative in the ways associated with parental psychological control. Parents' concern for their children's safety in dangerous neighborhoods often takes precedence over giving their children more freedom. Research on adolescents in dangerous neighborhoods finds a major strategy employed by parents is *not* allowing their children to have so much freedom (Furstenberg et al., 1998; Sampson et al., 1997). As Furstenberg and his colleagues found, "In general, African-American parents were more engaged in family management strategies that minimize danger and maximize opportunity than white parents, regardless of socioeconomic status. They were more inclined to protect their children from street influences by restricting their freedom, taking measures to confine them to the household after school and on weekends" (1998, p. 142).

In fact, Boykin and Allen's (2001) study of adolescents in both low- and high-risk contexts found *negative* developmental outcomes for teens in high-risk communities who are more autonomous. While they found social competence benefits for low-risk teenagers who exhibited autonomy, teenagers in high-risk environments who exhibited autonomy reported increased levels of delinquent activity. Boykin and Allen hypothesize that this is due to a combination of the many opportunities surrounding teenagers in high-risk contexts to engage in deviant behavior and the absence of other, safe opportunities to gain autonomy. In high-risk contexts, the natural developmental process of adolescent autonomy seeking is often blocked or misdirected. Boykin and Allen report, "High-risk teens may have fewer opportunities to gain autonomy from a part-time job, scholastic success, or extra-curricular activities, and thus for these teens, problematic behavior may be one easily accessible arena through which they can assert themselves and gain independence" (2001, p. 232).

In view of all this sometimes conflicting research, one recommendation seems in order for parents trying to respond to their children's autonomy needs when safety is an issue. Given that more-than-ideal regulation or *behavioral* control measures may be required, parents should try to support their adolescents' *psychological* autonomy as much as possible. This means including them in shared decision-making, talking with them about issues and supporting their problem solving and personal planning efforts, and connecting them to community resources where they can do service to others.

While several studies have made a good case for the differing effects of warmth, rules/expectations, and decision-making power in promoting health and academic achievement (Herman et al., 1997), a consistent conclusion from the literature is that all three family protective factors are important, albeit, perhaps in different proportions, not only to different cultural groups but based on individual and *contextual* differences as well. It remains for the parent or family caregiver to keep all three protective factors in a dynamic balance depending on the specific child and the specific context. This means loving our kids and using our intuition and common sense to keep regulations and rules from becoming a form of emotional control. Perhaps it is up to each parent or family caregiver to consider the following questions from Brooks and Goldstein: "When you interact with your children, do you ask yourself if they are gathering strength from your words and actions? When you put your children to bed at night, do you think about whether they are stronger people because of the things you have said or done that day? Have they gathered strength from you that will reinforce their sense of self-worth and resilience?" (2001, p. 88).

Family support programs acknowledge the family as the child's first and foremost environment.

FAMILY RESILIENCE

A growing movement over the last decade has been that of family support programs, which attempt to redress the limitations of a "narrow focus on individual resilience [that] has led clinicians to attempt to salvage individual 'survivors' without exploring their families' potential, and even to write off many families as hopeless" (Walsh, 1998, p. 23). Family support programs see that the best and most effective ways to foster resilience in youth is to foster it in the family caregivers. This approach acknowledges the family as the child's first and foremost environment and is based on nurturing family resilience as well as the resilience of individual family members. In the vignette reported by Katy Butler (1997) below, it is clear, for example, that Patty Tachera's children also benefit from the personal strengths she has developed with the help of a family support program:

> Late last summer, at a table in the cafeteria of Kauai Community College, Connie Bunlaga, a carefully dressed, white-haired older Filipina woman, was holding Patty Tachera's hand. Connie is Patty's support worker from Healthy Start. Patty, 41, is a single mother now studying to be a teacher. Her only island relatives are the four children she is raising alone. Born in Florida, she was 20 when she followed a surfer friend to Hawaii and stayed on. She married a man who beat her and, later, their son and daughter. After eight years she fled, only to have two sons with another, emotionally abusive man. Her daughter, now in her early teens, has not beaten the odds: she is living in therapeutic foster care because of her uncontrollable violence

toward Patty and the other children. Patty signed up for Healthy Start and met Connie two years ago, shortly after giving birth to her youngest son. "I had a one-year-old and a newborn and no support," she says. "I lived through the men in my life. I was overweight. I cried all the time. I couldn't sleep. You get so low you can't pick yourself back up. In a very mellow, calming way, Connie kicked me in the butt."

Over the next year, Patty experienced the sort of upward spiral that characterizes the lives of resilient children who meet good mentors. Connie came to see her every week. Patty lost 30 pounds.... Patty decided to become a teacher and went back to school; Connie helped her get aid from a state rental subsidy program. Finally, Patty kicked out her emotionally abusive boyfriend.

"She's like my mother," Patty says.... "She has a calming effect on me.... I don't think I was ever happy before, but I am now," she continues, "I'm much more patient with the babies. I don't find myself yelling as much. It's so important to have somebody who you know cares about you."

Treating the family as the unit of change, family support programs apply to the family the protective approaches for nurturing individuals — caring, high expectations, and opportunities for participation (Patterson, 2002; Walsh, 1998) — recognizing that many of the resilience strengths found in young people can be tapped in families as well (Benard, 1997).

A wonderful aspect of the family support movement is that these hundreds of family support programs are incredibly diverse, arising locally but applying global resilience principles. While family support programs look different structurally — and range from family centers to programs that are part of larger organizations such as Boys and Girls Clubs, to organizations that infuse family support principles into their mission, to community-level systems of care in which family support sites form an integrated network of care, to actual comprehensive community collaborative structures that plan and organize human services at the community level (Diehl, 2002) — they are all based on caring relationships between staff and family, high expectation beliefs that the family not only has strengths to nurture but also has innate resilience and the capacity to grow and change, and that the most effective way to work with families is through a strengths-based approach, a partnership with them that welcomes their gifts and contribution (Family Support America, 2000; Schorr, 1997). The Family Support Network (http://www.familysupport.org), for example, lists the following principles for Family Support Centers:

- The relationship between program and family is one of equality and respect.

- Participants are a vital resource.

- Programs are community-based and culturally and socially relevant to the families they serve.

- Parent education, information about human development, and skill building for parents are essential elements of every program.

- Programs are voluntary — seeking support and information is viewed as a sign of family strength.

Evaluations of family support programs, such as of California's Healthy Start, consistently document positive adult and child outcomes from these efforts (Wagner & Golan, 1996). A meta-analysis of 665 studies representing 260 programs, the 2001 National Evaluation of Family Support Programs, computed effect sizes (a statistical measurement that allows comparison of results across studies) for nine possible outcomes, including the major goals of these programs — improved parenting and enhanced child development. While a short summary follows, an overall finding of this evaluation is that program quality matters — it's how we do what we do that ultimately makes the difference. Researchers found that effect sizes *doubled* when the programs used family support best practices (Layzer at al., 2001) (see Table 1).

The family support field, like most others in the human services, has faced increasing pressures for accountability over this last decade. According to the Harvard Family Research Project, probably the major source of knowledge for the family support field, two other major assessment projects are underway: the National Family Support Mapping Project and the Promotional Indicators Project. The former is an effort to locate and collect information on every family support program in the country and to create a comprehensive national database that would answer "simple but important questions: How many family support programs are there? What families are they serving? What are the services and programs being offered? What are the funding sources for these programs?" (Diehl, 2002, p. 14). The latter project will develop indicators for measuring family strengths and capacities, instead of using deficit-based indicators that measure the negative aspects of families.

Evaluations of family support programs consistently document positive adult and child outcomes.

Table 1. Effects of Best Practices in Family Support Programs

Selected Variables of the 2001 National Evaluation of Family Support Programs	Effect Size When Variable Was Present in the Program	Effect Size When Variable Was NOT Present in the Program
Children's Cognitive Development Outcomes		
included an early childhood component	.48	.25
targeted to special needs children	.54	.26
peer support opportunities for parents	.40	.25
parent groups rather than home visits	.49	.26
Children's Social and Emotional Development		
parent self-development was a program goal	.56	.25
professional staff used rather than paraprofessionals	.43	.27
Parenting Attitudes and Knowledge		
peer support opportunities for parents	.33	.17
targeted to children with special needs	.57	.18
Parenting Behavior		
parent self-development was a program goal	.42	.24

It is to be hoped that with all of this assessment activity, the family support field can form a viable lobby for social and economic policies that support families and children. A recent finding with dire implications for children's well-being is that mothers participating in the welfare-to-work programs of the last several years display twice the rate of clinical depression — two mothers in every five — compared to the general population. According to these researchers, "Maternal depression sharply depresses their young children's development" (Fuller et al., 2002). Given that the 2001 meta-analysis discussed above found a positive long-term effect size of .39 for family economic self-sufficiency, it seems likely that a family support approach would provide a more developmentally supportive, resilience-enhancing, and, in the long run, economically viable approach to helping families in poverty. Moreover, it would offer the strong possibility of creating a healthy next generation, one reflecting the most powerful protective factor in a child's development — having a quality care-giving experience in the family (Werner & Smith, 2001).

[*Family Protective Factor Indicators* are found in Appendix B.]

CHAPTER 6
School Protective Factors

One of the most important and consistent findings in resilience research is the power of schools, especially of teachers, to turn a child's life from risk to resilience (Garbarino, 1992; Garmezy, 1991; Higgins, 1994; Masten & Coatsworth, 1998; Rutter et al., 1979; Werner, 1996; Werner & Smith, 1982, 1992). While much of the recent research about effective schooling focuses on students' academic performance, the role of schools in young people's lives is clearly broader than pedagogy and more important than test scores. Especially in the absence of positive family relationships, schools can provide an alternative source of protective, nurturing support. As one appreciative young adult remembers, "School was my church, it was my religion. It was constant, the only thing that I could count on every day.... I would not be here if it was not for school" (*Children's Express,* 1993).

On the other hand, when schools fail students, these young people could not be more at risk. The National Longitudinal Study of Adolescent Health (Add Health) found school failure to be the single strongest predictor of adolescent risk, so strong that they label school failure a "public health problem" (Blum, Beuhring, Shew et al., 2000).

THE QUALITY OF THE SCHOOL ENVIRONMENT

What characterizes a school environment that promotes young people's resilience? No long-term, controlled study has emerged that quite compares with Michael Rutter and his colleagues' (1979) classic investigation of high-poverty schools over twenty years ago. His study to determine what characteristics of schools produced positive and negative outcomes in students was significant in documenting not only how schools can protect or fail to protect students from risk, but also that the effects of such approaches are cumulative. Rutter found that problem behaviors in youth declined more the longer students were in nurturing schools and increased more the longer they were in non-nurturing schools.

One promising study, recently undertaken by the Project on High Performing Learning Communities, which has over the years involved more than 1,500 schools, 60,000 teachers, and 1 million students, is looking at students' academic outcomes in addition to their health and well-being. The critical question for the project researchers is "How do we create educational contexts in which all children and youth are nurtured and challenged in ways that lead them to be highly effective learners, achieve and perform at high levels, and be healthy, responsible, and productive citizens in our democracy" (Felner, 2000, p. 283). The comprehensive, developmental framework guiding this project matches very closely the framework advocated in this document and applies it to the adults in the school as well as to the students. Strategies being tested parallel much of what is advocated in this chapter: Small learning communities; a core academic program; high expectations for all students; empowering decision-making for students, teachers, and administrators; professional development; fostering health and safety for all student and school community members; engaging families in the education of their students; and creating strong school-community and school-work linkages. The investigators so far have found that students who were in schools that had more fully implemented these strategies achieved at much higher levels than those in non-implemented schools and substantially better than those in partially implemented schools (p. 291).

The characteristics of a well-functioning learning community as defined above by the Project on High Performing Learning Communities are mirrored in the resilience models of a number of education approaches — holistic education (R. Miller, 1995), progressive education (Meier, 1995, 2002), invitational learning (Purkey, 1995), partnership education (Eisler, 2000), additive schooling (Valenzuela, 1999), relational learning (Pariser, 2001), developmental education (H. Gardner, 1993, 2000), confluent education (Brown, 1990), intrinsic motivation (Deci, 1995; Kohn, 1999) — to name a few. What resilience research offers advocates of each of these approaches is well-documented support for an educational approach based on meeting young people's basic psychological needs — for belonging and affiliation, a sense of competence and meaning, feelings of autonomy, and safety. As we'll see, schools and teachers that focus on the social, emotional, and spiritual (in terms of purpose and meaning), as well as on the cognitive, are transformative, helping all their students, no matter what their risks, develop social competence, problem solving, a sense of autonomy, and plans and hope for the future.

One of the richest areas of research in the last decade has looked at how children and youth of non-dominant cultural and linguistic groups succeed in school despite the barriers they continue to face (Ayers & Ford, 1996; Delpit, 1995; Ladson-Billings, 1994; Nieto, 1992, 1994; Sleeter & McLaren, 1995;

Swadener & Lubeck, 1995; Valenzuela, 1999). What is especially compelling about this research is that most of it is ethnographic, growing out of the personal narratives of the youth themselves and reflecting the principle that marginalized groups need to have a voice. The research directly explores what it means to young people of non-dominant groups to have or not have critical social capital — in this case the protective factors in school of caring relationships, high expectations, and opportunities for participation. Depending on the quality of the school environment, the outcomes for these students range from high engagement and college attendance to dropout rates of up to 75 percent.

Related to school environment and dropout rates, the Project on High Performing Learning Communities found that reorganizing high schools into small, developmentally supportive communities (120 or fewer students) for core academic subjects and providing a teacher-advisor for each student reduced school dropout rates 40 to 50 percent or more (Felner, 2000). It isn't surprising that this kind of school organization, which promotes relationships and seeks to avoid the alienation associated with large, impersonal schools, would be salutary. As the National Longitudinal Study of Adolescent Health (Add Health) found, feeling connected to school — operationalized as feeling "close to people at school," "happy to be at this school," "like I am part of this school," that "the teachers at this school treat students fairly," and that "I feel safe in my school" (Resnick et al., 1997) — was the most powerful protective factor of any school attribute studied, for all health risk behaviors, including violence.

In view of their parallel findings about the importance of family "connectedness" (discussed earlier), the Add Health researchers point out, "It is clear that when demographic characteristics are controlled, social contexts count. Specifically, we find consistent evidence that perceived caring and connectedness to others is important in understanding the health of young people today. While these findings are confirmatory of other studies, they are also unique because they represent the first time certain protective factors have been shown to apply across the major risk domains" (Resnick et al., 1997, p. 830).

Another large-scale study validating the importance of social contexts was the Center for Substance Abuse Prevention's National Cross-Site Evaluation of High-Risk Youth Programs (Sale & Springer, 2001). This five-year study of 48 sites found "Strong bonding with school and family show the greatest associations with reduced substance use for these youth at risk" (p. 7). In this study, school bonding or connectedness (youths' perceptions that school is a positive and rewarding environment in which they can succeed) was even more powerful a protective factor than family bonding.

Reorganizing high schools into small, developmentally supportive communities and providing a teacher-advisory for each student reduced dropout rates 40 to 50 percent or more.

How connected with their schools are students? It seems to depend on how old they are. Add Health researchers found that "The average level of school connectedness in all schools [n=127] is 3.64 on a scale from 1 to 5, indicating most students in most schools feel quite attached to school" (McNeely et al., 2002, p. 144). Barber and Olsen (1997), however, are less sanguine. Their longitudinal research explored children's and adolescents' perceptions of their socialization experiences in families, with peers, and in communities, as well as in schools. They found that while a large majority of youth reported very positive socialization experiences in their families and with their peers, where school was concerned, a majority reported negative socialization experiences, "characterized by decreasing levels of connection and regulation across the transition to middle school and low levels of psychological autonomy experienced in the classroom" (p. 297). An analysis by the ACT Office of Policy Research (Wimberly, 2002) using data from the NELS (National Educational Longitudinal Study), found that African American students experience these caring relationships with their teachers to a far less degree than do white students.

An age-related drop-off in school connectedness is also indicated by data from the California Healthy Kids Survey (WestEd, 2002). This survey of 270,000 students (as of Fall 2002) in grades 7–11 indicates that as students get older, school protective factors diminish across the board — as measured by caring relationships (i.e., connection), high expectations (positive beliefs in youth's capacities), and meaningful participation (psychological autonomy experiences).

CARING RELATIONSHIPS IN SCHOOLS

Resilience research tells all of us concerned with schooling and education that engaging each student's intrinsic motivation is key. It is by meeting young people's basic psychological needs to experience belonging and safety, to gain competence, to feel what they are learning is meaningful, and to develop autonomy that schools can tap this intrinsic motivation. Caring relationships with teachers and peers not only meet students' affiliation needs, but also lend support when learning tasks are difficult or uninteresting. It's no secret that children and adolescents will learn more readily from people they trust and respect, and in places where they receive trust and respect. It is a rare student who is incapable of learning what our schools have to teach. The challenge is for schools to engage and support the young people in their charge.

Resilience research conducted by the National Longitudinal Study on Adolescent Health (Resnick et al., 1997) and the national evaluation of Big

Brothers Big Sisters mentoring programs (Tierney et al., 1995) demonstrate that relationships are the key both to preventing health-risk behaviors and successfully engaging students' intrinsic motivation to learn. A point we must remember is that caring is as critical to adolescents as it is to younger children. A Stanford University study of adolescents from diverse socio-economic and racial groups found "The number of student references to wanting caring teachers is so great that we believe it speaks to the quiet desperation and loneliness of many adolescents in today's society" (Phelan et al., 1992, p. 698). Furthermore, studies of school dropouts repeatedly identify the lack of anyone who cared about them as students' main reason for leaving school (Croninger & Lee, 2001; Hamovitch, 1996; Loutzenheiser, 2002; Stevenson & Ellsworth, 1993). Researchers involved in the Collaborative for Academic, Social, and Emotional Learning (CASEL) argue that "Social and emotional development and the recognition of the relational nature of learning and change are the fundamentals of human learning, work, and accomplishment. Until this is given proper emphasis, we cannot expect to see progress in making schools safer, drug-free, with fewer students who don't care and want to drop out, or with better tolerance of people who are different" (Elias & Weissberg, 2000, p. 264).

When Teachers Care

A common finding in resilience research is the power of a teacher, often unbeknownst to him or her, to tip the scale from risk to resilience. Werner found that "Among the most frequently encountered positive role models in the lives of the children…, outside of the family circle, was a favorite teacher. For the resilient youngster a special teacher was not just an instructor for academic skills, but also a confidant and positive model for personal identification" (2000a, p. 126). Throughout the resilience literature, young people talk about teachers who listen, who notice when they are absent, and who seem interested in them. For example, a former student at Central Park East Secondary School describes an assistant principal who made an extra effort to be a male role model for a group of boys: "At times, he would pull us out of class, one by one, and walk us around the block and just talk. It was sort of, 'How have you been? How's everything at home? How's your mother? How's your brother?' That kind of support" (Bensman, 1994, p. 62).

Repeatedly, these turnaround teachers/mentors are described as providing, in their own personal styles and ways, the three protective factors (Benard, 1996; Deiro, 1996; Ladson-Billings, 1994; Moorman, 2001). They are identified, first and foremost, as caring. They convey loving support

A point we must remember is that caring is as critical to adolescents as it is to younger children.

— the message of being there for a youth, of trust, and of unconditional love. According to Baumeister and Leary's (1995) research on belonging, the best strategy for meeting the need to belong is unconditional acceptance. This does not mean relaxing expectations, however. When students are asked to define the qualities they want in their teachers, the answer, across studies, is unequivocal: They want teachers who are caring and who also accept no excuses — who, in other words, care about them enough to refuse to let them fail (Wasley et al., 1997; Wilson & Corbett, 2001).

Loving support also translates into meeting emotional safety needs. Resilient survivors talk about teachers' "quiet availability," "fundamental positive regard," and "simple sustained kindness" — a touch on the shoulder, a smile, a greeting (Higgins, 1994, pp. 324–25). Sandy McBrayer, founder of an alternative school for homeless youth and 1994 National Teacher of the Year, says, "I never judge.... I tell my kids I love them every day" (Bacon, 1995, p. 44).

At Central Park East, one of the three guiding principles of the school is that relationships be based on caring, respect, and mutual trust (Meier, 1995). According to the school's founding principal, Deborah Meier, respect, having a person "acknowledge us, see us for who we are — as their equal in value and importance" figures high in turnaround relationships and schools (p. 120). A parent from Central Park East explains what respect looked like in that school: "The teachers talked to the children like they were people, not just pupils that had to sit down and follow rules and regulations, and not really express themselves because there wasn't enough time with 40 children in a class. It wasn't like that. They took time with those children. They treated them as people" (Bensman, 1994, p. 57).

When Schools Create a Caring Climate

While we've only discussed teacher/student relationships, resilient outcomes are also associated with caring relationships among teachers, between teachers and family members, and among students (Pianta, 1999). For example, a growing body of psychological and developmental literature is finding positive peer relationships to be one of the most critical and influential forces in individual outcomes (Bearman et al., 1999; Harris, 1998). Over a decade of research by the Developmental Studies Center in Oakland, California, has documented the power of caring school and classroom communities in promoting positive developmental outcomes in students — and their teachers (Battistich, 2001; Battistich et al., 1995; Watson & Ecken, 2003). Likewise, three decades of research on the Yale Child Study Center's School Development Program (also known as the "Comer process") have found positive academic and behavioral outcomes in children when schools are developmentally focused and relationship-driven (Comer, 2001; Comer et al., 1996). Two researchers of Chicago school reform have also found that schools with high levels of "trusting" relationships among members of the school community outperform on standardized tests, including reading and math tests, those with low levels of trusting relationships (Bryk & Schneider, 2002).

Research studies of caring school and classroom communities point to a number of elements that promote students' innate resilience:

- *Every student has a caring relationship with adults at his or her school.* Many adults who work in schools naturally develop close relationships with some of the students. But to ensure that all youngsters have a positive and personal interaction with an adult at school, some schools take a more deliberate approach, specifically matching each student to an adult, including janitors, cooks, and bus drivers. These people make a point of checking in with their students at least once a week.

- *Schools and classrooms feel like communities.* Such environments embody a set of core values in teacher and peer relationships — mutual respect, responsibility, fairness, and helping (Battistich et al., 1997). The popular Tribes approach to creating physically and emotionally safe classrooms is based on similar values, which are incorporated into a set of classroom agreements for respectful behavior (Gibbs, 2001). Fostering school and classroom communities in which students feel safe, psychologically and physically, is increasingly being identified as a key role for the adults in a school (Bearman et al., 1999; Harris, 1998).

- *Schools and classrooms make use of a number of small-group processes.* These approaches, which allow students to practice the values of caring communities, include cooperative learning, peer tutoring, cross-age tutoring, service learning, conflict mediation, and peer support programs. In such student-to-student relationships, young people build empathy and experience themselves both as caring and cared for. These processes have been found to promote broad positive developmental outcomes — social-emotional, moral-ethical, and cognitive-academic (Johnson & Johnson, 1989; Pringle et al., 1993; Ryan, 2001). They have also been found to be *the* critical component of effective prevention programs, reducing alcohol, tobacco, and other drug use (Perry, 1989; Tobler, 2000), and school violence (Johnson & Johnson, 1996).

To ensure that all youngsters have a positive and personal interaction with an adult at school, some schools take a deliberate approach.

Peer helping and peer support programs have been successful in elementary, middle, and high schools in reconnecting disruptive and alienated students, as well as in building inclusion and a sense of belonging with new, immigrant, and English learner students and among racially, ethnically, and physically different students (Eggert et al., 1994; Tindall, 1995). (For further discussion of small-group processes, see page 82.)

- *Schools and classes are small.* Compared with large classes and schools, small ones provide greater opportunity for students, teachers, and other school staff to get to know one another. Documented results of smaller school environments include positive developmental and academic outcomes (Felner, 2000; Finn et al., 2001; Wasley et al., 2000). Recent analysis of the Add Health data found that small school size had a direct and positive relationship to students' sense of connectedness at school: As school size decreases, school connectedness increases (McNeely et al., 2002).

- *Caring relationships among school staff are encouraged and supported.* Relationships among the adults in a school — relationships between and among teachers, support staff, and administration — establish a climate that students also experience. We know that teachers naturally are more caring when they feel cared for themselves (Halford, 1998–99). We also know that when teacher collegiality is encouraged and thrives, students achieve better academically (McLaughlin & Talbert, 1993, 2001; Talbert & Wallin, 2001). Structures that support this collegiality include team teaching, reflective practice groups, peer support groups, and peer problem-solving groups (Palmer, 1998; Sergiovanni, 2000).

- *Discipline is designed to keep students feeling connected.* For example, instead of out-of-school suspensions and other strategies that tend to *dis*connect students, more positive approaches, such as "restorative justice," attempt to keep students connected to their school and classmates and build their sense of responsibility. Strategies based on this philosophy include peer-run "peacemaking circles," peer courts, and peer/staff/family conflict mediation (Bilchik, 1998).

- *Early intervention services are available.* Counseling, support groups, and student assistance programs provide the learning supports that are very often critical to helping students stay in school and achieve academically. These services demonstrate to students that their school cares, especially for those who are struggling (Barrera & Prelow, 2000; Eggert et al., 1994). These services typically involve the school in interfacing with student services professionals, social services providers, community-based organizations, law enforcement officials, and business and community leaders.

- *School-based mentoring programs link students with community volunteers.* Well-run mentoring programs yield positive health, social, and academic outcomes. In a controlled study of Big Brothers Big Sisters programs with over 1,000 youth, half of whom were matched with a mentor for 18 months, the mentored youth were found to be significantly less likely to initiate alcohol or drug use or skip school or class, and they showed improvements in their family and peer relationships and school grades (Tierney et al., 1995) (see also pp. 93–94). Hundreds of schools have now created such programs, linking community volunteers with students in after-school programs (Sipe & Roder, 1999). In fact, school-based mentoring programs are now the most prevalent form of mentoring (Herrera et al., 2000).

- *Families and the community are invited to partner with the school.* Schools can reach out to create positive relationships with their students' families and with community agencies. A school, for example, can serve as the location for a family resource center, which might provide such services as peer support groups, parent education, child care, and teen parenting classes. Or it could become a full-service community school, housing a full range of human services and programs for students and their families in the after-school hours. Such partnerships generate a sense of belonging within the broad school community, and they are associated with positive developmental outcomes and achievement motivation in students (Comer et al., 1996; Dryfoos, 1998; McDonald & Moberg, 2000; Schorr, 1997).

HIGH EXPECTATIONS IN SCHOOLS

At the core of caring relationships are clear and positive expectations that not only structure and guide behavior but also challenge students beyond what they believe they can do. During the last *two* decades, research on successful schools and programs for youth in challenging circumstances has clearly demonstrated that high expectations — with concomitant support — is a critical factor in decreasing the number of students who drop out of school and in increasing the number of youth who go on to college (Mehan et al., 1994; Meier, 1995). According to a historical review of teacher expectations by Rhona Weinstein (2002), "Across multiple studies, teachers appear to provide those students for whom they hold high expectations more opportunities to learn, and under more positive conditions, than for students for whom they hold low expectations" (p. 51). High expectations are also a common characteristic of "high-performing, high-poverty" schools (James et al., 2001).

When teacher collegiality is encouraged and thrives, students achieve better academically.

Expectations are communicated to students in several ways according to expectancy communications theory. Weinstein and her colleagues at the University of California, Berkeley, provide a conceptualization especially helpful to this discussion. They claim that expectations — either high or low — are communicated to students not only through relationships and messages but also through the structure, organization, curriculum, and practices of schools (Weinstein, 2002; Weinstein et al., 1991; Weinstein & McGown, 1998).

When Teachers Communicate High Expectations

As we've already discussed, a teacher is a powerful communicator of messages. A winning message is one that challenges students: "You can do it," "You have what it takes to succeed in this classroom and school," "You have what it takes to achieve your goals and dreams," and "The world is tough out there, and you have to be tougher" (Delpit, 1996, p. 200). These and other authentic interpersonal expectations reflect the teacher's deep belief in the student's innate resilience and self-righting capacities.

Powerful teachers are strengths-based and student-centered. They use students' own experiences, strengths, interests, goals, and dreams as the beginning point for learning, competence, and accomplishment. Thus, they tap students' intrinsic motivation, their existing, innate drive for learning. At Central Park East, where college-bound students increased from 15 to 85 percent of the student body in three years time (Bensman, 1994), "Teachers helped students develop pathways to learning, starting from interests students brought from home or discovered in the classroom" (p. 7). In follow-up interviews, graduates recounted "over and over again…that their teachers provided the support and encouragement they needed to discover an interest and develop a skill; as they developed and became recognized for a skill, their self-esteem improved, and they took on greater academic challenges" (p. 6).

High expectation teachers become turnaround teachers by recognizing students' existing strengths, mirroring them back, and helping students see where they are strong. They especially assist those overwhelmed youth who have been labeled or oppressed by their families, schools, and/or communities to understand their personal power to *reframe* their life narratives from damaged victim to resilient survivor. Turnaround teachers help youth see the power they have to think differently about and construct alternative meanings for their lives. (See Seligman's model for shifting youths' perspectives on page 31.)

It goes without saying that high-expectation educators do not *label* their students — as "at risk" or anything else. Educator Herb Kohl says, "I have never taught an 'at-risk' student in my life.... It defines a child as pathological, based on what he or she might do rather than on anything he or she has actually done" (Nathan, 1991, p. 679). Instead of anticipating failure, a consistent description of turnaround teachers is their ability to see students' possibilities. Lisa Delpit recounts this characteristic in terms of its importance to African American students: "Perhaps even more important than what our teachers taught us is what they believed. They held visions of us that we could never imagine for ourselves. And they held those visions even when they themselves were denied entry into the larger white world. They were determined that, despite all odds, we would achieve" (1996, p. 199).

When Schools Are Structured for High Expectations

While teachers have the power to communicate expectations, schools have the power to institutionalize them. Expectations structured by school programs and policies can be strengths-based or deficits-based, with predictable outcomes in each condition.

Conveying high expectation beliefs to all students flies directly in the face of tracking, a labeling and segregating practice that hangs on in schools despite *two* decades of scientific studies documenting its negative effects, especially for students from non-dominant linguistic and cultural groups (Nieto, 1992; Oakes, 1985; Olsen, 1998; Wheelock, 1992). As a National Research Council report indicates, "Assignment to low tracks is typically associated with an impoverished curriculum, poor teaching, and low expectations" (Heubert & Hauser, 1999, p. 5). In contrast, high-performing, high-poverty schools make college core classes available to all students who want to take them. A characteristic of schools that are closing the achievement gap is their refusal to dumb down or limit the opportunities for lower-achieving students (James et al., 2001).

Testing and assessment practices are another structural indicator of school expectations. High-stakes testing, an approach that has been called the "standardization of minds" (Sacks, 1999), appears to be particularly detrimental to resilience and youth development (Kohn, 2000; Meier, 2000; Ohanian, 1999; Popham, 2001; Sacks, 1999). The adverse effects of high-stakes testing on English learners has already been documented (Heubert & Hauser, 1999), and the case is mounting that high-stakes testing decreases students' connectedness to school, the major protective factor in adolescent health-risk behaviors (Blum & McNeely, 2002). Common sense alone tells us what a National

A characteristic of schools that are closing the achievement gap is their refusal to dumb down or limit the opportunities for lower-achieving students.

Research Council report concludes: "In the absence of effective services for low-performing students, better tests will not lead to better educational outcomes" (Heubert & Hauser, 1999, p. 3). As Weinstein concludes in her comprehensive study of the power of expectations in schooling, "The art of knowing, appreciating, and learning from children's unique and diverse talents has been all but lost from a culture of schooling that focuses narrowly on the point differences on standardized tests. We can and must do better if we wish to take seriously the essential tenet at the heart of education: helping each child become all that she or he can become" (2002, p. 303).

While our education systems have, by and large, adopted an overly narrow definition of success and the areas in which success is important, research into "multiple intelligences" by Howard Gardner (2000) and his colleagues at Harvard University provides a powerful alternative for guiding strengths-based practice in schools. By identifying categories of abilities or strengths — what they refer to as "intelligences" — that are common to all human beings but that vary in degree in each person, these theoreticians and researchers highlight the range of opportunities for human beings to be "successful" — including in the areas of verbal/linguistic, logical/mathematical, visual/spatial, bodily/kinesthetic, musical, naturalistic, interpersonal, and intrapersonal. These intelligences, especially the inter- and intrapersonal, map well to Daniel Goleman's (1995) traits of emotional intelligence and the personal resilience strengths discussed in chapter 2.

Assessment practices that acknowledge this broader range of human potential for success try to measure students' unique strengths, interests, and accomplishments. Additionally, authentic assessments, such as student portfolios, performance tasks, and student exhibitions that are directly tied to student learning, convey a high-expectation message that the student is truly the constructor of knowledge and meaning (Cooper, 1997).

Conveying these high expectations means that schools and classrooms do not simply recognize and mirror back strengths but actually provide opportunities for their further development. In other words, high-expectation schools offer multiple and varied opportunities for success to all students. Student-centered high expectations certainly mean one size does *not* fit all (Ohanian, 1999). To ensure that students develop a sense of personal competence, which is both a basic psychological need and an attribute critical to life success, high-expectation schools employ a number of strategies described below.

- *Instruction is individualized to accommodate the broad range of students* — their different intelligences, learning styles, life experiences, personal strengths, interests, and goals. Individual Education Plans (IEPs), used most commonly with special education students, can serve as a helpful mental model here (Levine, 2002). Whether written formally in partnership with parents and students (more of a possibility in small classes than in large ones) or existing "virtually" in a teacher's head (as they do for most good teachers), a careful inventorying of a student's strengths and needs keeps instruction student-centered.

- *Learning opportunities are structured so that success is possible.* This strategy, closely related to individualized learning, entails matching the subject matter to the readiness of the student to learn it: The student must be challenged yet able to achieve success. In itself, providing students with learning activities that are neither too easy nor too hard for them lets them know that you understand and care about them.

- *The curriculum is rich with art, music, and outdoor experiences and projects.* Research shows that experiences in these areas can generate positive youth development and contribute to school success (Catterall, 1997; Hattie et al., 1997). Too often, however, art, music, and outdoor experiences are stripped from the curriculum when resources are tight, denying students whose special intelligences are visual/spatial, musical, or naturalistic these opportunities to excel.

- *Students have a choice of interest-based after-school clubs.* Such clubs allow students to explore their interests, expand their knowledge, and hone their skills in small groups with other like-minded individuals. These clubs and programs are open to all students who want to participate.

As part of recognizing each student's unique strengths, high-expectations education capitalizes on students' life experiences and cultural contexts. Not only do students find their experiences and cultures embedded in rather than "decorating" the curriculum, but their teachers understand that how children learn is influenced by the basic organization of their culture, namely toward collectivism or individualism. For example, cooperative learning and helping will be a lot more natural for students from a culture that emphasizes and values interdependent relations and the well-being of the group than for students from an individualistic culture that emphasizes individual fulfillment and choice (Trumbull et al., 2001). Teachers and parents are considerably more effective partners when they recognize how their cultures may differ (Trumbull et al.). In *Subtractive Schooling: U.S.-Mexican Youth and the Politics of Caring,*

Teachers and parents are considerably more effective partners when they recognize how their cultures may differ.

Angela Valenzuela (1999) documents the range of adverse effects for students when their cultures are not valued or respected.

As Valenzuela found, and as Lisa Delpit concurs, the expectations communicated to students whose home language is not English should "validate students' home language without using it to limit students' potential. Students' home discourses are vital to their perception of self and sense of community connectedness.... The point must not be to eliminate students' home languages, but rather to add other voices and discourses to their repertoires" (Delpit, 1996, p. 205). This point is also made by the President's Advisory Commission on Educational Excellence for Hispanic Americans (2000). This commission cites research by Garcia and Otheguy (1995) as follows: "When majority educators look at the education of Hispanic children in the United States, they focus on their linguistic deficits.... Those of us in public education need to learn...that bilingualism and biliteracy are obtainable if one holds both children and teachers unequivocally responsible for obtaining them." The report goes on to note that "the context of a child's home culture is essential...and that continuity with the intellectual and social climate of the home is of paramount importance if the school is to help children develop and foster their intellectual and social growth" (pp. 99–100). Not surprisingly, resilience research associates positive lifetime outcomes for youth who develop cross-cultural competence (Gandara, 1995).

In addition to holding high expectations for *what* students will learn, high-expectation schools are also concerned with *how* students think. Schools that encourage the resilience strengths critical thinking and inquiry and the development of a critical consciousness are not only able to more effectively engage youth but are especially effective at communicating the expectation that students are truly capable of complex problem solving and decision-making (Kohl, 1994; Mehan et al., 1994). One of the most cited turnaround schools of the last decade, Central Park East, organized the entire curriculum around developing critical consciousness. Students were taught to ask five questions of everything they were learning, questions designed to create critical "habits of mind": How do we know what we know? Who's speaking? What causes what? How might things have been different? and Who cares? (Meier, 1995).

Developing a critical consciousness also means making racism, sexism, ageism, heterosexism, discrimination, bullying, and harassment an explicit part of the curriculum so that students can explore these issues that are so salient to all of their lives. The resilience strength of critical consciousness is based not only on understanding the "ism" but on developing skills in confronting it as well. Developing critical consciousness around the mass media and advertising has been shown to be a particularly effective strategy in alcohol, tobacco, and teen pregnancy prevention programs (Kilbourne, 1999).

One last aspect of expectations is that of having fair and equitable rules for behavior in the classroom and school. Unfair and inequitable discipline policies and procedures are continually cited by students in focus groups as a major area for school improvement. The Add Health researchers found inequitable discipline policies to be associated with disconnecting from school (Blum & McNeely, 2002). Additionally, classrooms and schools that set behavioral expectations without student input, according to Alfie Kohn's (1996) examination of school disciplinary and classroom management procedures, reflect what he sees as the fundamental problem with most discipline and most education: a lack of belief in children's capacities. Unless educators have a positive belief, that is, high expectations, about children's capacities, they will not be able to provide the third protective factor, opportunities for young people to be active participants in and contributors to their school community.

OPPORTUNITIES FOR PARTICIPATION AND CONTRIBUTION IN SCHOOL

Creating the opportunities for student participation and contribution is a natural outgrowth of working from a strengths-based perspective. It is through having the opportunities to be heard in a physically and psychologically safe and structured environment — to voice one's opinion, to make choices, to engage in active problem solving, to express one's imagination, to work with and help others, and to give one's gift back to the community — that youth develop the attitudes and competencies characteristic of healthy development and successful learning: social competence, problem solving, autonomy, and a sense of self and future.

Especially critical to developing healthy psychological autonomy, young people need the opportunity and freedom to grow, make decisions, and safely meet challenges *within* the structure of a safe and caring environment to which they feel connected. This connection between autonomy and belonging is mutually reinforcing: the stronger someone's sense of self, the more able he or she is to form healthy connections to other people, with those healthy connections, in turn, further nurturing the sense of self.

Research has found that students who experience autonomy-supportive school environments are more likely to be curious, mastery-oriented, problem solvers, intrinsically motivated, and committed to democratic values, in addition

As early as preschool, and with lifelong effects, students benefit from school practices that promote self-control.

to having a higher sense of self-efficacy (Barber & Olsen, 1997; Chirkov & Ryan, 2001; Deci, 1995; Ryan & Deci, 2000). Participating in decisions about one's life and future is one of the major ways humans meet their fundamental need for autonomy and power. Several education reformers believe that ignoring this need — not only of children but also of family members, teachers, and the school staff — makes schools alienating places (Glasser, 1990; Kohn, 1996; Sarason, 1990). If data from California's young people is representative, by the time students get to the 11th grade, only 16 percent of them feel that they have opportunities to "help decide things like class activities or rules," "do interesting activities," and "do things at school that make a difference" (http://www.wested.org/hks). Seymour Sarason's classic quote says it simply: "When one has no stake in the way things are, when one's needs are provided no forum, when one sees oneself as the object of unilateral actions, it takes no particular wisdom to suggest that one would rather be elsewhere" (1990, p. 83).

Youth who feel a sense of their own autonomy and power in the context of a caring school community also develop self-control. Alfie Kohn's review of the research on student decision-making leads him to conclude that "It is in classrooms and families where participation is valued above adult control that students have the chance to learn self-control" (1993, p. 18).

As early as preschool, and with lifelong effects, students benefit from school practices that promote self-control. Longitudinal evaluations of the preventive intervention, the High/Scope Educational Research Foundation's Perry Preschool Program (Schweinhart & Weikart, 1997c), found positive personal, social, and economic outcomes for adults who had attended a preschool program based on active participation and child-initiated learning. In contrast, adults whose preschool experience had been one of direct instruction and teacher control — whose self-control was not promoted — paid a price later in life: They dropped out of high school at higher rates, had lower incomes, and were much more likely to be repeat offenders. Echoing the findings by Brian Barber (2002) and others about the effects of highly controlling family environments, the Perry Preschool researchers warn: "Our study suggests that when children experience a heavily unilateral atmosphere, their sociomoral actions and underlying reasoning are less advanced than when children experience a more reciprocal atmosphere" (Schweinhart & Weikart, 1997c, p. 12).

Schools that give students opportunities for autonomy and control use approaches such as the following:

- *Students experience "voice and choice" in their daily life at school.* The most important factor in developing autonomy is having a reasonable degree of personal control, which in this case means ensuring appropriate opportunities for students to make decisions throughout the school day. For example, allowing students some choice in terms of what they read and what they write about is an effective approach for developing literacy as well as autonomy. Assessment processes that are authentic and participatory, such as portfolios, help students develop self-awareness and metacognition — the empowering ability to think about their thinking. When students have meaningful responsibilities in the classroom, such as for creating the class governing rules and holding regular class meetings, they develop the skills and attitudes of responsible citizenship. Similarly, when a problem develops in the classroom or on the schoolyard, inviting student ideas about how to address it, either through whole class discussion or a student focus group process (see below) signals respect for students' ability to act responsibly.

Sonya Nieto's research about successful students from a wide variety of ethnic, racial, linguistic, and social-class backgrounds identified listening to students as the key strategy for educational change, one which is too often ignored: "Student perspectives are for the most missing in discussions concerning strategies for confronting education problems. In addition, the voices of students are rarely heard in the debates about school failure and success, and the perspectives of students from disempowered and dominated communities are even more invisible" (1994, p. 396).

Infusing the power to make choices and decisions into the life of the classroom (or school, community organization, after-school program, treatment program, and so on) does not necessarily require any special programs, but it does require adults to let go of a control orientation, to see young people as a valuable resource, to willingly share power with them, and to create a system based on reciprocity and collaboration rather than on control and competition.

- *Students have many experiential learning opportunities.* These are essential for developing student autonomy and power. Experiential learning takes many forms and names: arts-based learning, project-based learning, service-learning, career/technical apprenticeship, outdoor adventure learning, and cooperative learning, to name a few. The components of experiential learning include hands-on learning activities, group learning that is supervised or facilitated by adults or older youth, and time for self- and group-reflection. Research has found that learning in the context of experience builds student autonomy and power and promotes all the other categories of resilience

> Inviting student ideas about how to address a classroom or schoolyard problem signals respect for students' ability to act responsibly.

strengths as well, including social competence, problem solving, and sense of purpose (Hattie et al., 1997). Experiential approaches provide opportunities for learning that is meaningful to students.

- *Group process is infused throughout the curriculum and school day.* This means extensive use of cooperative learning, student focus groups, and community circles. It is difficult to imagine a structure that better embodies all three protective factors — caring relationships, high and clear expectations, and opportunities for participation and contribution — than a small group with a common focus. As noted previously, research does not disappoint us in validating the power of group process, i.e., peer-to-peer interaction. Such approaches promote positive academic outcomes and diverse developmental outcomes, including positive cross-cultural and cross-differences relationships (Eccles & Gootman, 2002; Johnson & Johnson, 1989; Slavin, 1990, 1995; Tobler, 2000).

Cooperative learning is an especially salient group process since it can easily be used across the curriculum and at all grades. In this pedagogical approach, hetereogenous groups of students work together to achieve a shared learning goal. Effective cooperative learning tasks are designed to require positive interdependence and a feeling of mutuality. Students must experience even marginalized students as contributors to the group, which may necessitate the teacher assigning some students specific tasks based on their strengths (Cohen, 1994). Cooperative learning tasks must also be designed to ensure that students experience interactions that build their interpersonal and small-group social skills. Responsibility for the group process and products occurs both on the individual as well as the group level, with time for reflection about how the group worked together built into the task.

Since research began on this process in the early 1970s, the International Association for the Study of Cooperation in Education claims that over a thousand studies now corroborate the power of this educational intervention to produce holistic developmental outcomes — cognitive, emotional, social, moral, and spiritual (in terms of meaning and purpose). In studies with matched control groups, researchers have found the following benefits of cooperative learning: increases in academic scores, empathy, social skills, motivation, acceptance of diversity (ethnic, racial, physical), conflict resolution, self-esteem, self-control, positive attitudes toward school, and critical thinking (Aronson, 2000; Johnson & Johnson, 1989; Slavin, 1990,

1995). According to Robert Slavin, "What is remarkable is that each of several quite different methods has been shown to have positive effects on a wide variety of outcomes.... In general, for any desired outcome of schooling, administer a cooperative learning treatment; about two-thirds of the time there will be a significant difference between the experimental and control groups in favor of the experimental group. Rarely, if ever, will differences favor a control group."

Another kind of group process, the student focus group, provides students with authentic ways to contribute to the life of their school by dealing in an ongoing way with school problems and issues and by providing feedback about school climate (Nieto, 1994). As a school reform process, the School Change Collaborative, a network of staff members from 10 federally funded regional education laboratories, school practitioners, and other education stakeholders, developed *Listening To Student Voices*, a toolkit designed to increase the role of students in continuous school improvement. As the authors of the toolkit point out, "Schools should use this process to identify ways to make the school better by learning what their students really think.... It is an important data-gathering tool that also serves to increase student responsibility and teacher motivation for school improvement." (Laboratory Network Program, 2000, p. 4).

Student focus groups — along with parent and teacher focus groups — were found by Mary Poplin and her colleagues to be transformative in reforming schools. As they reported in *Voices from the Inside* (Poplin & Weeres, 1992), "The difference in the way participants on these campuses [the one middle and one high school and the two elementary schools in the study] feel about themselves and others suggest to us that the processes we initially used for research purposes may be extremely important for the transformation of individual schools and the transformation of our teaching practices" (p. 44). They documented, for example, that education issues, such as the achievement gap and teacher flight stem from an underlying lack of caring relationships, low expectations, and lack of opportunities to participate and be heard. "Relationships dominated all participant discussions about issues of schooling in the U.S. No group inside the schools felt adequately respected, connected, or affirmed" (p. 19). Given everything we know about resiliency, it should be no surprise that "students, over and over again, raised the issue of care. What they liked best about school was when people, particularly teachers, cared about them or did special things for them" (p. 19).

Student focus groups provide students with authentic ways to contribute to the life of their school.

These researchers concluded, "Defining a process whereby the people inside schools can work continuously through the transformation of their own school site must become a priority. It is a national paradox that a nation whose ideological roots are so profoundly democratic would structure an education system that valued the teaching about democracy but not its practice" (p. 39).

Educational change guru Michael Fullan also weighs in on the participation issue: "Educational change, above all, is a people-related phenomenon for each and every individual. Students, even little ones, are people, too. Unless they have some meaningful (to them) role in the enterprise, most educational change, indeed most education, will fail. I ask the reader not to think of students as running the school, but to entertain the following question: What would happen if we treated the student as someone whose opinion mattered in the introduction and implementation of reform in schools?" (1991, p. 170).

Another process for inviting participation and contribution is through a community circle process called "council." Council is designed to allow each member to experience listening and being listened to about issues of deep personal importance (Kessler, 2000; Zimmerman, 1996). While this is a common process in community-based youth programs, it can also be incorporated into the school as part of a prevention or early intervention program, in a health or social-emotional living class, or in an after-school program. The council process was developed by Jack Zimmerman (1996) and has been expanded into a social-emotional literacy curriculum by Rachel Kessler (2000) called "Passages," which deals with salient adolescent issues, such as friendship, communication skills, stress management, diversity, study skills, problem solving, health, and personal and social responsibility. Unlike most prevention programs, however, "Passages" also addresses adolescents' deep yearnings for connection, identity, and meaning.

- *Students have many opportunities to express themselves through the arts.* Students are encouraged to explore and share their thoughts, ideas, or concerns in theater, dance, photography, video production, art, music, storytelling, creative writing, and/or memoir writing. Several national, large-scale research studies have found that, regardless of their education and economic backgrounds, young people involved in the arts, either in their schools or through community-based organizations, do better academically, socially, and behaviorally (Fiske, 1999).

For example, UCLA researcher James Catterall's (1997) analysis of data from the National Educational Longitudinal Survey of over 25,000 middle and high school students involved in the arts shows that they do better than students with little or no arts involvement in a number of significant ways: academically and on standardized test scores, on persistence in school, and on a sense of commitment to the community. In a later analysis of 62 studies of various categories of arts programs by nearly 100 researchers, Catterall found diverse gains once again, in academic achievement, on standardized tests, in social skills, and in student motivation (Henry, 2002). According to Catterall, the research suggests that "Arts education may be especially helpful to poor students and those in need of remedial instruction" (Henry, 2002).

- *Students have opportunities for community service learning.* This approach integrates students' academic learning with service that meets real-world needs, allowing students to experience themselves as active contributors making a difference in their community (National Commission on Service Learning, 2002). What makes service learning so powerful is the partnership that is created among young people, their teachers, and community adults as they work toward the shared goal of community improvement — a process now known as *community youth development.* Several statewide evaluations, along with the national evaluation of Learn and Serve programs across the country, have documented academic and developmental benefits for students, with effects related to engagement in school, grades, core subject GPA, educational aspirations, personal responsibility, social responsibility, acceptance of cultural diversity, and leadership (Melchior, 1996, 1998; RPP International, 1998). Moreover, these evaluations found positive effects for teachers, school climate, community attitudes toward young people and their schools, and community betterment. Similarly, an experimental evaluation with random assignment of the nationally replicated Teen Outreach Program found significant reductions in teen pregnancy, school failure, and academic suspensions with the 342 program youth compared to the 353 control group youth (Allen et al., 1997). School-based community service was a major component in this youth development program.

- *Students have a way to take active responsibility for transgressions.* Finally, replacing retributive discipline practices with restorative practices gives students who have wronged others ways to make amends. "Restorative justice," a movement led this past decade by the University of Minnesota especially, is a resilience-based approach to discipline that moves away from punishment toward restoring a sense of harmony and well-being for all who have been affected by a hurtful act. It provides families, schools, and communities a way to ensure accountability while at the

Replacing retributive discipline practices with restorative practices gives students who have wronged others ways to make amends.

same time breaking the cycle of retribution and helping those involved to unlearn violence. Common forms include peacemaking circles, teen courts, peer and staff mediation, conflict resolution programs, family group conferencing, and classroom constitutions. A critical aspect of this approach is that it keeps a young person in relationship with others rather than isolating or stigmatizing him or her. Early evidence suggests the power of this approach to promote positive developmental, prevention, and academic outcomes (Bilchik, 1998).

RESILIENT SCHOOLS

A way to think about resilient schools is to recognize the structural risk factors such schools have avoided or overcome and the protective factors they have in place. For example, we now see research on "high-performing" or "high-flying" schools. These are schools that are successfully serving those students most often left behind in education improvement efforts — Latino, African American, Native American, and low-income students. Resilient schools are made up of students whose innate resilience is promoted rather than dampened by the people and conditions they encounter there. Nel Noddings's classic observation reminds us that positive youth development and successful learning are not competing goals: "At a time when the traditional structures of caring have deteriorated, schools must be places where teachers and students live together, talk with each other, take delight in each other's company. My guess is that when schools focus on what really matters in life, the cognitive ends we now pursue so painfully and artificially will be achieved somewhat more naturally.... It is obvious that children will work harder and do things — even odd things like adding fractions — for people they love and trust" (1988, p. 32).

"High-poverty" schools where students have mastered fractions and much more are not anomalies. Researchers have found, just as they did with individuals exposed to high-risk environments, remarkable success in the face of extreme challenges. Nearly half of the 4,500 schools across the country that were identified as "high-poverty" and/or "high-minority" (African American and Latino) scored in the top third of all schools in their states, often out-performing predominantly white schools in wealthy communities (Jerald, 2001). The strengths that distinguish these high-performing, high-poverty schools match well to the protective factors identified repeatedly by resilience researchers (Baldwin, 2001; James et al., 2001; Jerald, 200l; MacBeath et al., 1995; Rutter, 1979; Scribner & Scribner, 2001; Wilson & Corbett, 2001).

Several other sources of research over this last decade also provide supporting evidence for the resilient school model presented here. Case studies with long-term follow-up of individual schools in high-poverty communities, such as Deborah Meier's Central Park East, Marva Collins's Westside Preparatory School, and the Community School in Maine (Bensman, 1994; Meier, 1995; Day, 1994; Safer, 1995), along with evaluations of processes, such as James Comer's School Development Program (Comer et al., 1996) or the Child Development Project of the Developmental Studies Center (Battistich, 2001; Battistich et al., 1995) weigh in with corroborative evidence that even schools with huge challenges can succeed for their students.

Many of the research-based strategies used by resilient schools are described in *Closing the Achievement Gap* (Williams, 1996/2003). These include school-linked services and resources for urban communities and families; making urban schools and classrooms culturally compatible with students' home backgrounds and conditions; having teachers who communicate high expectations, caring, and cultural sensitivity; giving urban students opportunities to learn; creating school environments that foster students' resilience; and fostering high levels of teacher engagement.

Schools that are able to move from risk to resilience are characterized along a number of dimensions in Figure 5. Any school that finds itself to the right side of this chart can be considered a resilient school — at its essence a true community where teachers, families, and students connect through caring relationships, communicate positive beliefs about each other, and invite each other's participation in a shared vision that *all* children are *our* children.

For too long, the emphasis on academic and behavioral outcomes that has driven education and prevention policy and programs has all but ignored the question of just *how* these outcomes will be achieved. Given the evidence of brain science research and resilience research that every person has the capacity for learning and healthy development (except in the case of severe central nervous system damage), how this will happen is an issue of engagement and motivation. How do schools engage these innate capacities? How do we tap students' intrinsic motivation to learn? How do we encourage their low-risk health behaviors? As the approaches and programs in this document demonstrate, the answer requires a shift in the fundamental paradigm of education and prevention — a shift from the paradigm of control to the paradigm of development. The road to both positive learning and healthy behavior is through the process of meeting young people's developmental needs.

[*School Protective Factor Indicators* are found in Appendix C.]

The fundamental paradigm of education and prevention must shift from control to development.

Figure 5. Moving from Risk to Resiliency in Our Schools*

From Risk	To Resiliency
Relationships Between and Among Teachers, Students, Parents	
Blaming, controlling, hierarchical	Caring, encouraging, participatory
Teacher Behavior and Attitudes	
Looks for deficiencies "This work is required. You may not be able to do it. You're on your own."	Looks for strengths in each student "This work is important. I know you can do it. I won't give up on you."
Physical Environment	
Dirty, peeling paint, graffiti Windows, toilets, etc. broken No displays of student work Only sports trophies displayed	Clean, fresh paint, no graffiti Windows, toilets, etc. well maintained Student work on display Varied examples of student achievement
Curriculum and Instruction	
Fragmented, non-experiential Eurocentric focus Limited access to college core/enriched courses Limited variety of courses and activities Narrow range of learning styles accommodated Behaviorist approach, status-quo thinking	Integrated, experience-based/service learning Cultures of all students reflected College core/enriched courses available to all Broad variety of courses and activities Broad range of learning styles accommodated Constructivist approach, inquiry-based/critical thinking
Grouping	
Homogeneous, tracked Individual competition Pull-out programs Large, anonymous schools and classrooms	Heterogeneous, untracked Cooperative groups Integrated programs Schools within schools, small schools and classrooms
Evaluation	
Standardized Few intelligences measured Focus on "right" answers	Authentic, multiple measures Range of intelligences measured Focus on fostering self-reflection
Learning Motivation	
Competitive Extrinsic rewards No meaningful student engagement about content	Collaborative Intrinsic rewards Active student engagement connecting learning to interests, strengths, and real world
Discipline	
Authority-determined rules Punitive No student involvement in meaningful decision-making	Democratic, consensual norms and rules Restorative Active student participation in decision-making

*Adapted from Weinstein et al., 1991.

CHAPTER 7
Community Protective Factors

During the last decade, much has been written about the breakdown of community and neighborhood life — and the loss of social capital, the linkages that create a sense of belonging and identity, and, in Emmy Werner's words, "that give meaning to one's life and a reason for commitment and caring" (Bellah, 1992; Putnam, 2000; Werner & Smith, 1982). The late John Gardner warned, in fact, that "The forces of disintegration have gained steadily and will prevail unless individuals see themselves as having a positive duty to nurture their community and continuously reweave the social fabric" (1991, p. 11).

Harvard's Robert Putnam (2000) pulls together data from several national surveys to show that Americans have become increasingly disconnected — from family, friends, neighbors, and social organizations. In *Bowling Alone: The Collapse and Revival of American Community*, he documents the threat this shrinking social capital poses across the board and especially to our most vulnerable populations — children, youth, and young families. Probably a majority of Americans, and most scholars, would agree with Putnam's thesis that "Our schools and neighborhoods don't work so well when community bonds slacken, that our economy, our democracy, and even our health and happiness depend on adequate stocks of social capital" (p. 28). Most of us would likely also agree that problem behaviors we are so concerned with — alcohol and other drug abuse, domestic and youthful violence, crime and delinquency, early pregnancy, and child abuse — share as a root cause the loss of these critical social networks and the opportunities for healthy development that they represent. As Marian Wright Edelman has argued for more than three decades in her role as founder and president of the Children's Defense Fund, "It really takes a community to raise children, no matter how much money one has. Nobody can do it well alone. And it's the bedrock security of community that we and our children need" (1991, p. 32).

THE POWER OF COMMUNITY

Longitudinal studies during this last decade indicate that while the absence of a strong community is devastating for young people, the reverse is also true: positive community contexts can be transformational (Carnegie Task Force on

Youth Development and Community Programs, 1992; McLaughlin, 2000; McLaughlin et al., 1994; Werner & Smith, 1992). Werner and Smith (1992), for example, documented the power of relationships and opportunities in the community to be protective for youth and young adults from troubled families and schools. In surveys of over 100 communities, the Search Institute found that while caring and supportive families make a major difference in the lives of their own youth, caring and support in the community were especially protective for youth with few family and school resources (Blythe & Leffert, 1995). Milbrey McLaughlin and her colleagues' 10-year study of over 60 neighborhood-based organizations serving over 24,000 urban youth made the same discovery: Quality neighborhood organizations, they report in *Urban Sanctuaries: Neighborhood Organizations in the Lives and Futures of Inner-City Youth,* were turnaround places for youth, especially for those who had not received the critical protective factors in their families and especially in their schools (McLaughlin et al., 1994). Additionally, experimental design studies employing random assignment have found the power of these neighborhood–based organizations to connect young people to a bright future. For example, the community-based Quantum Opportunities Program serving poor adolescents in poor neighborhoods through a comprehensive youth development-based program found program youth outperforming control group youth not only academically but in life skills as well (Hahn et al., 1994).

Adding to this research is a growing body of studies that emanate from the MacArthur Foundation's research networks, including The Project on Human Development in Chicago Neighborhoods. Over a period of eight years, ending in 2002, project researchers collected data in 343 Chicago "neighborhood clusters," or "communities." The analysis of this data is ongoing. Primary among the study purposes is to understand the social dynamics in a community that contribute to promoting or preventing youthful crime and disorder. "Collective efficacy" is the term researcher Robert Sampson and his colleagues (Sampson et al., 1997) use to describe communities where residents consistently interact in ways that are positive and cooperative. As Sampson explains, "It's a sense of shared expectations among neighbors. It's the social networks people have, the values that they share and whether or not they trust each other" (Owens, 2002). When these characteristics exist, regardless of a community's poverty level, neighbors look out for the young people in the community, hold them to "orderly" behavior, and take collective action — for example, to get rid of a local drug hangout. The Chicago neighborhoods researchers reported that rates of violence differed dramatically in poor communities with similar demographics, depending on the level of collective efficacy. Nonviolent communities were characterized as providing the critical protective factors of caring relationships, high and clear expectations, and opportunities for participation to their children and youth (Sampson et al., 1997).

As tantalizing as the community efficacy research may be for the future, the decade's most influential focus on youth and their communities has been that of youth/adolescent development, a movement defined by its emphasis on meeting young people's developmental needs. Karen Pittman, the visionary leader of the youth development field, first at the Center for Youth Development and Policy Research at the Academy for Educational Development and later through the International Youth Foundation's Forum for Youth Investment, has, with her colleagues, documented a decade's worth of youth development work with community-based youth organizations and translated it into recommended practices and policies for youth organizations, foundations, states, and federal agencies (Pittman & Irby, 1998).

In reflecting on the decade, Pittman and colleague Merita Irby credit two reports, each published by a foundation commission in the late 1980s, with helping to jumpstart the youth development movement — *Turning Points: Preparing American Youth for the 21st Century,* by the Carnegie Task Force on Education of Young Adolescents (1989), and *The Forgotten Half: Pathways to Success for American's Youth and Young Families,* by the William T. Grant Foundation Commission on Work, Family, and Citizenship (Halperin, 1988).

These reports emphasized the need to support the development of two previously ignored populations — early adolescents and late adolescents, especially late adolescents not bound for college. A third report, *A Matter of Time: Risk and Opportunity in the Nonschool Hours,* by the Carnegie Task Force on Youth Development and Community Programs (1992), drew further attention to a previously ignored context for development — out-of-school or nonschool hours in the community.

Pittman and Irby cite these reports, in concert with Benard's resilience research synthesis (1991), Benson's survey research at the Search Institute, and the National Longitudinal Study of Adolescent Health (discussed earlier) as critical research supporting youth development and "the argument that the best way to prevent problems is not to narrowly reduce risks, but to broadly strengthen the individual, family, and community assets that young people have in their lives" (Pittman & Irby, 1998, p. 162).

Regardless of a community's poverty, a sense of shared expectations among neighbors results in "collective" efficacy.

Intentional approaches to "reweave the social fabric" to support young people have taken several forms: informal family-school-community partnerships, focused efforts to build effective community/neighborhood-based organizations, and more extensive community-wide or system-wide collaboration efforts (often called comprehensive community initiatives or CCI's).

Several major community-wide initiatives based on a resilience/youth development model have emerged, sponsored mainly by foundations, such as Annie E. Casey, Ford, California Wellness, Kellogg, and Rockefeller — to name just a few — but also by collaboration at the federal level with departments, such as SAMHSA (Substance Abuse and Mental Health Services Administration), education, and juvenile justice. Three models of community change are especially important to note in terms of their resilience/assets/youth development approach: the Healthy Communities/Healthy Youth initiative of the Search Institute, Asset-Based Community Development, and Community Health Realization.

The Search Institute, under the leadership of Peter Benson, has worked in hundreds of communities this last decade to create "asset-promoting communities" focused on providing young people with 40 critical developmental assets associated with healthy development and life success (P. Benson, 1997; Blyth & Roehlkepartain, 1993).

The Asset-Based Community Development Center at Northwestern University, under the leadership of John Kretzmann and John McKnight, has also worked for more than a decade on "inside-out" community-building, with a special focus on bringing in marginalized citizens, including young people.

Community Health Realization, led by Roger Mills, has worked intensively in communities throughout the U.S. to help "reconnect people to the health in themselves and then direct them in ways to bring forth the health in others. The result is a change in people and communities which builds up from within rather than is imposed from without" (Mills, 1993, p. 6).

In these, as in all comprehensive community initiatives, evaluation poses a major challenge. A two-volume series, *New Approaches to Evaluating Community Initiatives: Concepts, Methods, and Contexts* (Connell et al., 1995; Fulbright-Anderson et al., 1998), produced by The Aspen Roundtable on Comprehensive Community Initiatives (CCIs), which was established early in the decade in response to the burgeoning interest in CCIs, testifies to the issues and challenges of documenting outcomes in such complex social change interventions. According to Michelle Gambone, "Community change initiatives, as is clear to everyone associated with them, are very complex endeavors. Whatever the particular focus of individual initiatives, all CCIs have in common the ambitious goal of catalyzing and sustaining significant change in fundamental aspects of social, economic, and political structures and their functioning in communities" (1998, p. 149).

No matter which approach is examined, however, as discussed below, an effective community or multi-system intervention depends, just as an effective school or family one does, on the quality of relationships; the beliefs about children, youth, and families; and the opportunities children, youth, and families have to be active partners in the process.

CARING RELATIONSHIPS IN THE COMMUNITY

One of the major findings from resilience research is the power of informal mentors — neighbors, friends' parents, teachers, or anyone who takes the time to care — as protective factors in youth's lives. This aspect of social capital, especially in local neighborhoods, has been one of the great casualties of contemporary life. The Search Institute's surveys of hundreds of communities have found only a minority of youth reporting sustained, inter-generational relationships with non-parent adults (Benson, 1997). Given this great unmet need, researchers have been very curious to find out whether planned mentoring relationships could fill this role. The field can now answer with confidence. Using an experimental design and a randomly assigned control group, a scientifically exemplary national evaluation of Big Brothers Big Sisters of America (Tierney et al., 1995), the country's best known mentoring effort and one of three programs considered a model youth development program by the Institute of Medicine (Eccles & Gootman, 2002), found that 18 months after 571 treatment youth were matched with adult mentors from the community — compared to 567 control group youth who were not — these young people were significantly less likely to use illegal drugs, to drink, to hit someone, or to skip class or school, and they were making modest gains in their grade-point averages. Moreover, the mentored youth improved their relationships with both their parents and their peers relative to their control counterparts.

Besides establishing the power of caring relationships in the community, this evaluation also definitively establishes a youth development/resilience approach as the most effective form of prevention: These findings are

Three models of community change are especially important to note: Healthy Communities/ Healthy Youth of the Search Institute, Asset-Based Community Development, and Community Health Realization.

stronger than those from most traditional alcohol and other drug or violence prevention efforts, even though this intervention had nothing explicitly to do with prevention. In the words of the researchers, "The findings in this report speak to the effectiveness of an approach to youth policy that is very different from the problem-oriented approach that is prevalent in youth programming. This more developmental approach does not target specific problems, but rather interacts flexibly with youth in a supportive manner (Tierney et al., 1995, p. 1).

A companion study of Big Brothers Big Sisters, *Building Relationships with Youth in Program Settings* (Morrow & Styles, 1995), examined the nature of the relationships that produced these positive outcomes. The sustained relationships were those in which the mentor saw himself or herself as a friend, not as a teacher or preacher out to "fix the kid." These relationships were grounded in the mentor's belief that he or she was there to meet the developmental needs of youth — to provide supports and opportunities the young person did not currently have. These volunteers placed top priority on having the relationship be enjoyable and fun for both partners. They were "there" for the young person, listened nonjudgmentally, looked for the young person's interests and strengths, and incorporated him or her into the decision-making process. Of these relationships, 93 percent met consistently, and 91 percent were ongoing at the end of the 18 months (compared to 29 percent and 32 percent of the "prescriptive" relationships). This latter finding documents that fostering resilience is not about a program per se, not even a program like mentoring. Rather, it is about the *quality* of relationship, it is about *how* we do what we do.

Caring relationships characterize transformational youth-serving neighborhood-based organizations (NBOs) as well (Catalano et al., 1999; Ferguson, 1990; Freedman, 1993; Gambone & Arbreton, 1997; McLaughlin, 2000; McLaughlin et al., 1994; Weitz, 1996). In their cross-site study of turnaround NBOs, or "urban sanctuaries," McLaughlin and her colleagues consistently found youth workers who knew how to connect with youth and draw out their best. While these successful youth workers differed on almost all visible dimensions (race, ethnicity, gender, etc.), they all shared fundamental characteristics essential to creating programs that work with youth. Their number-one priority — and a distinguishing characteristic of successful youth development programs — was that youth needs come before the needs of the organization, the program, or an activity. As one of the youth workers in the study stated, "This focus matters enormously in the barren, harsh neighborhoods of the inner city, where youth test leaders' commitment and caring at every turn and where what is normal is often unpredictable and brutal. For inner-city youth, a leader's being always available and responsive to daily realities supersedes the content of any program" (McLaughlin et al., 1994, p. 99).

The Institute of Medicine's recent review, *Community Programs to Promote Youth Development* (Eccles & Gootman, 2002), names "supportive relationships" as one of the key characteristics of community settings that produce positive youth outcomes and ascribes the following interrelated qualities to these settings: an atmosphere of warmth, connectedness, good communication, and support; adults who provide secure attachments, are good mentors and managers, and provide scaffolding for learning; adults whom youth experience as caring and competent and loving or "cool." This report further reminds us that there is "not one perfect type of adult for all adolescents and all settings.... Inasmuch as there is an underlying essential element here, it consists of attentiveness and responsiveness to adolescents' subjective worlds" (p. 95).

In successful youth-serving community organizations, fostering caring relationships among peers is also a primary goal. Besides an adult who can be counted on, young people need to experience a sense of belonging to a group (Eccles & Gootman, 2002; Werner & Smith, 1992). Each of the caring strategies described in the school section of this document apply to community-based organizations as well (see pages 68–73). Additionally, community youth-serving organizations have traditionally done a much better job than schools in designing programs to be welcoming to adolescents from multiple cultural groups; cultural inclusiveness is often a primary goal of these programs. According to the Institute of Medicine report, the following elements are necessary to building inclusion in a community program:

- Interactions between groups must be on a level of equal status;

- Activities must be cooperative rather than competitive, involving pursuit of a shared goal;

- There must be individualized contact between members of groups;

- Institutions and authority figures must support the goal of intergroup understanding; "Institutional silence," an atmosphere in which race is

Besides an adult who can be counted on, young people need to experience a sense of belonging to a group.

never mentioned, can lead to unspoken perceptions of discrimination and intergroup tensions. Group differences must be acknowledged; and

- Adults have important roles, as "role models, pathfinders, arbitrators, peacemakers, interpreters, mentors, promoters of civic ethics, and administrators" (Eccles & Gootman, 2002).

Even at the wider community level, healthy communities and successful community collaborations/change efforts to support youth depend on the quality of relationships between people. The Rockefeller Foundation's report on successful community initiatives concluded that "While community building is more an art than a science, research shows that relationships are key to turning lives around.... Building on this insight to develop networks of social support in low-income neighborhoods cannot help but yield positive change" (Walsh, 1997). Robert Sampson and his colleagues found in their Chicago neighborhoods research that communities that were willing to intervene in the lives of other people's children, that is, communities that shared the belief that all children were *their* children, had lower levels of violence than other demographically similar communities. Moreover, they found that "At the neighborhood level, the willingness of local residents to intervene for the common good depends in large part on conditions of mutual trust and solidarity among neighbors" (Sampson et al., 1997, p. 919).

Similarly, three of the previously cited resilience-based approaches to building healthy communities to promote positive youth and human development — Asset-Based Community Development, Healthy Communities/Healthy Youth, and Community Health Realization — emphasize building caring relationships.

Kretzman and McKnight's Asset-Based Community Development model of community change holds that because feeling disempowered is one of the major results of people's growing disconnection from each other, the first step in empowerment is reconnecting through relationships. They write, "The sense of efficacy based on interdependence, the idea that people can count on their neighbors and neighborhood resources for support and strength, has weakened. For community builders who are focused on assets, rebuilding these local relationships offers the most promising route toward successful community development" (Kretzman & McKnight, 1993, p. 10).

From the perspective of Peter Benson, leader of the Search Institute's Healthy Communities/Healthy Youth initiative, caring relationships have always been the way cultures have "passed on the best of human wisdom — through wisdom modeled, articulated, practiced, and discussed by adults with children around them. It is learning through engagement with responsible adults that nurtures value development and requires intergenerational community" (P. Benson, 1997, p. 93). Noting that increasingly these responsible adults are paid to be with young people, Benson hopes to counter "an increased sense that one has to be professionally trained in order to be effective in caring for youth — or for that matter, to contribute to community life" (p. 92).

Community Health Realization is another community change model that provides an antidote to Benson's concern. Program facilitators start with creating caring and respectful relationships with individuals in the community so that these community members, in turn, become the actual change agents (Mills, 1993).

In sum, no matter whether we look at informal or formal mentoring relationships in the community or at relationships experienced through neighborhood organizations or community-wide change efforts, the heart of community lies at the relational level, and any attempt to rebuild a sense of community connection for youth must begin with caring relationships.

HIGH EXPECTATIONS IN THE COMMUNITY

High expectations in the community take place on several levels: in the community generally, in community youth-serving organizations, and through community initiatives. High expectations in the community can also be discussed in terms of how they are framed: as beliefs about children and youth's capacity, as clear expectations and guidance for behavior, and as youth-centered/strengths-focused messages and activities.

The loss of community relationships among adults and between adults and youth increasingly means that nonparenting adults in the community no longer know youth, no longer share norms for young people's behavior, and no longer are willing to share responsibility for other people's children. When they no longer know and interact with children and youth on a regular basis in the community, surveys confirm that they are much more likely to adopt anti-children/anti-youth attitudes. Surveys by Public Agenda, a nonpartisan, nonprofit public opinion research and education organization, consistently found throughout the 1990s that about two-thirds of the adults polled had only negative attitudes toward adolescents ("rude," "irresponsible," "wild," etc.), and, even more disturbing, nearly half of those polled had a negative view of young children (Public Agenda, 1997).

> **When adults no longer know and interact with children and youth on a regular basis in the community, surveys confirm that they are much more likely to adopt anti-children/anti-youth attitudes.**

Young people talk about adults who cross the street to avoid passing them or of adults who refuse to talk to them or even make eye contact.

Researcher and youth advocate Mike Males (1996, 1999) has written passionately about this anti-youth sentiment, especially the role of the media and policymakers in "scapegoating" American youth. Males methodically takes every "myth" perpetuated about adolescents and documents with hundreds of studies that each of these is truly a myth, including, for example, "Teens are violent thugs," "Teens need more policing," "Teens are druggie wastoids," "Teen moms are ruining America," and so on (1999).

Unless community adults get to know and develop relationships with their young people, they remain vulnerable to negative stereotypes and convey messages to children and youth that they are not valued. While young people talk about adults who cross the street to avoid passing them or of adults who refuse to talk to them or even to make eye contact, the most devastating message to American youth over this last decade has been society's willingness to incarcerate them at levels unheard of in other civilized societies.

On the other hand, we know there are communities — including poor communities — where adults do know their young people, do look out for them, and do have shared, high expectations for their behavior (Sampson et al., 1997).

The power of shared community expectations was identified in a 10-year study conducted by Francis Ianni and his colleagues at Teachers College, Columbia University, and reported by Ianni (1989) in *The Search for Structure: A Report on American Youth Today*. While Ianni's report probably presents a more optimistic picture of community norms than similar research might find a decade later, it nonetheless yields some valuable insights and findings that can guide intentional efforts to rebuild community to support children and youth, especially during their transition to adult status.

The Teachers College research team observed and interviewed thousands of adolescents in the many contexts of their lives — families, schools, peer groups/gangs, youth programs, street corners, and even jails — in 10 geographically, racially, ethnically, and socio-economically representative communities throughout the U.S. Their guiding research questions were "What are the codes or rules that structure and organize the transition from child to adult status in the social context of actual communities, and how do the adolescents in these communities internalize and learn to use or abuse these rules?" (p. 7). Ianni's presentation of the findings clearly challenges the prevailing belief that adolescent society, or "youth culture," is a social system separate from the community. As he points out, "Adolescent development takes place within a specific community as the individual teenager's internal resources are nurtured or stifled by the opportunities available" (p. 23).

What made a difference for youth, Ianni found, was experiencing shared expectations in the context of relationships: "In every community, urban inner-city as well as suburban or rural, we found that not only age-mates but a variety of continuing relationships with family members, relatives and neighbors, institutional settings, and the significant adults who are part of them serve as exemplars and guides for individual or groups of adolescents. Congeniality among their values and clarity and consistency in their guidance are essential to the adolescent, who is engaged in a search for structure, a set of believable and attainable expectations and standards from the community to guide the movement from child to adult status. If the values expressed by different community sectors are at odds, if their directions are unclear or inconsistent, the teenager cannot be expected to accept their good will or trust their judgment" (p. 262).

Communities that worked well for adolescents were those in which adolescents were linked into positive social support systems with adult role models and with positive peers. Ianni calls for rebuilding this natural social fabric (i.e., social capital) along with creating a formal, planned "youth charter," which would define the expectations and standards that can meet the developmental needs of the adolescents in the community" (p. 279). This would be done through "comprehensive community planning" involving youth as well as other community members. Interestingly, the 1990s found neighborhood community-based organizations and community-wide collaborations rising to the challenge of providing high and clear expectations.

Investigations into successful youth-serving community-based organizations consistently find a sense of structure and safety as the critical foundation (Eccles & Gootman, 2002; Gambone & Arbreton, 1997; McLaughlin, 2000; McLaughlin et al., 1994). According to the Institute of Medicine report, "A key characteristic of successful community programs is that they have clear rules about expected behavior when in the program, and the staff are regularly involved in monitoring participants' behavior, even when youth are elsewhere" (Eccles & Gootman, 2002, p. 93).

Rules governing how members treat each other are especially critical. "Nothing negative" is a common agreement, McLaughlin found. "Members

Successful youth-serving community-based organizations consistently provide a sense of structure and safety as the critical foundation.

are expected to be supportive, fair, and keep close watch on the safety of the group. In groups with a span of ages, youth care for, mentor, work with, and induct younger members into the organization just as older sisters and brothers might" (2000, p. 15). The rules are also clear, fair, and "youth-centered in their flexible application" (p. 15). McLaughlin and her colleagues found that programs that encouraged the youth to help create the rules governing their behavior more readily engaged the trust and buy-in of the young people, exemplifying the maxim that people don't sabotage what they helped create. "All the successful programs we saw operate on the basis of a few rules that are based in the cultural authority of the group" (McLaughlin et al., 1994, p. 109). The critical issue for community organization caregivers, just as it is for family caregivers, is determining a level of structure that is "developmentally, ecologically, and culturally appropriate," a structure that permits "age-appropriate levels of autonomy" (Eccles & Gootman, 2002, p. 93).

Another aspect of high expectations in successful community organizations is what the adults believe about the capacities of their young people. For example, a transformational camp for youth, Camp Marwood, in Oak Park, Illinois, explains its staff members' common "awe, wonder, and respect for the wonderful, terrifying, and never-ending experience of growing up" and their commitment to help each young person "to be the best self they can be." Young people who experience such protective beliefs learn to respect and believe in themselves. According to *Urban Sanctuaries* (McLaughlin et al., 1994), the first and most elemental attribute of the successful youth worker is seeing the potential and not the pathology of youth, including disadvantaged youth. These youth workers operate from a resiliency perspective of having high expectations for their youth while also working from and playing to their young peoples' strengths. These characteristics are found in the successful mentors in the Big Brothers Big Sisters evaluation (Morrow & Styles, 1995) as well. For example, here is the voice of a developmentally oriented mentor: "[When he told me about a bad grade,] I kind of focused on his other grades first; he said that he had done a good job with the other ones. And then I asked him if he wanted to do better in it, and then I kind of asked him how he could do better. And it was a pretty simple thing because he just didn't do a couple reports. So we decided that the next ones he got I would help him with them if he wanted. And we did that twice. You know, it's like what can we do together to do this" (p. 59).

Because of their focus on potential and the positive, successful youth-serving programs do not label children and youth. They especially avoid labels "that mark youngsters as deficient or deviant and concentrate instead on raising expectations and providing settings where youth can gain the attitudes, confidence, and measure of expertise necessary to remove themselves from the inner city's despair" (McLaughlin et al., 1994, p. 97). Furthermore, "Successful leaders locate 'the problem' of inner-city youth and the dysfunctional behaviors and attitudes associated with them primarily in the larger society and the general failure of social institutions to understand, support, or care for these teenagers" (p. 97). Successful mentors similarly locate risk in an unsupportive environment, not in the youth themselves (Morrow & Styles, 1995). Having a youth-centered, strengths focus is another critical component of effective community organizations that convey high expectations. To be youth-centered means "talent-scouting," or being on the lookout for a young person's gifts, and also providing opportunities for each youth to discover and explore his or her interests, strengths, goals, and dreams.

When youth have the chance to develop skills that are relevant and meaningful to them, they are creating a bridge to that vital resilience strength, belief in a compelling future. In fact, a sense of hope and bright future is exactly what McLaughlin and her colleagues (1994) found in the youth they studied.

Successful initiatives that take an even broader, community-wide approach communicate high expectations through their positive beliefs in young people's and their families' capacities, focusing on strengths and assets. The starting point for Community Health Realization initiatives is to help individuals directly recognize their innate wisdom and resilience and develop a sense of self-efficacy, which, in turn, results in their feeling powerful and hopeful enough to take action with others to improve their community (Mills, 1993).

The approach of Asset-Based Community Development is to begin with a "community assets map." According to McKnight, "The starting point for any serious development effort is the opposite of an accounting of deficiencies. Instead there must be an opportunity for individuals to use their own abilities to produce. Identifying the variety and richness of skills, talents, knowledge and experience of people in low-income neighborhoods provides a base upon which to build new approaches and enterprises" (1992, p. 10). Creating a community assets map thus begins the process of neighborhood regeneration, which "locates all of the available local assets, begins connecting them with one another in ways that multiply their power and effectiveness, and begins

Creating a community assets map begins the process of neighborhood regeneration.

A growing body of research points to the power of arts-based community organizations. Similarly, an enormous amount of research points to the effectiveness of mentoring and community service.

harnessing those local institutions [and individuals] that are not yet available for local development" (Kretzmann & McKnight, 1993, p. 6).

OPPORTUNITIES FOR PARTICIPATION AND CONTRIBUTION IN THE COMMUNITY

In terms of providing young people with opportunities for participation and contribution, successful community organizations offer ongoing opportunities for youth to (1) build their competencies and skills through engaging, challenging, and interesting activities, including job training and apprenticeships for older youth; (2) build belonging through active participation in group process and with peers in small interest-based groups; (3) develop a sense of power and respect through problem solving and decision-making; and (4) find a sense of meaning through activities that incorporate dialogue and reflection while providing community service and contribution to others, including their peers (Gambone & Arbreton, 1997; McLaughlin, 2000; McLaughlin et al., 1994). As discussed in relation to school protective factors, these opportunities have all been shown to promote positive developmental outcomes — especially a sense of connectedness — and to reduce young people's involvement in problem behaviors (Hattie et al., 1997; Melchior, 1996, 1998; Resnick et al., 1997; RPP International, 1998; Sale & Springer, 2001). And as we saw in one-to-one relationships, the Big Brothers Big Sisters evaluation found that successful mentors were those who provided youth the above opportunities (Morrow & Styles, 1995).

Community organizations also benefit from the strategies described earlier for building meaningful youth participation in school settings, including the strategies of experiential learning, community circles, cooperative learning, focus groups, the arts, community service, and restorative justice disciplinary practices (see pages 79–86).

A growing body of research points to the power of arts-based community organizations. Recall that Shirley Brice Heath and her colleagues' study of these organizations found that youth involved in them did better academically, were less likely to drop out of school, felt a greater sense of self-efficacy, and were more likely to perform community service (Heath et al., 1998).

Similarly, an enormous amount of research points to the effectiveness of mentoring and community service — in community as well as school settings (Eccles & Gootman, 2002) — and is discussed below in terms of the growing community youth development movement.

Adventure programming (Outward Bound, ropes courses, and so on) is another especially effective approach used by community-based organizations. Hattie and his colleagues' (1997) analysis of over 96 adventure programs (involving 12,000 youth) found that youth made gains on 40 different outcomes, categorized into leadership, self-concept and self-control, academics, intrapersonal, interpersonal, and adventuresome. A key finding of this study is that the youth outcomes continued to increase over time, a sharp contrast to most educational interventions in which program effects fade after the program terminates. When effects continue or increase, it is reasonable to infer a turnaround intervention, a person, place, or experience that literally "turns" the course of a young person's development onto a positive path.

A *sine qua non* in creating effective community-wide initiatives for youth — and others — is engaging their active involvement. All resilience-based community change approaches have as a bottom line getting youth involved as partners in the change effort. Youth, just like adults, need to have ownership and active roles in the life of their community if the community is to serve as a protective factor (Kirschner et al., 2003).

Taking youth participation to its most fundamental level, community youth development (CYD), an emerging movement of the late 1990s, places the emphasis on youth themselves becoming community change agents, fully capable of improving their communities not only for young people but also for families and other community members. For example, the California Wellness Foundation funds community-based initiatives in which, according to foundation president Gary Yates, "Young people work in leadership roles alongside of adults to determine what changes are needed in their physical, social, and chemical environments to promote health and wellness in their communities" (*TCWF Newsletter*, 1999).

Ten of these wellness initiatives — which begin with a planning phase that enhances the skills of the adult and youth leaders, identifies community assets, and forms advisory councils (whose membership, like the leadership, include up to 75 percent young people) — have been funded for over a million dollars each, a strong vote of confidence in the concept of community youth development. The perceived benefits within these communities have included the personal growth of participants, a new source of powerful role models for young people, increased understanding and tolerance within the communities, and healthier communities. As Leah Johnson, a foundation advisory committee member says, "I don't know if [the adults] realize that we've gained a whole

Taking youth participation to its most fundamental level, community youth development places the emphasis on youth themselves becoming community change agents.

new perspective on the contributions they make.… It gives me hope that, even though it will take time, together we can make changes in our communities" (Cleland et al., 2001).

In contrast to other community development approaches, CYD holds that healthy communities cannot be built without a youth development approach, one that actively enlists young people in the change effort. The ultimate goal of this approach is the creation of "safe, just, prosperous communities, countries, and world where young people are partners and contributors working with adults to positively influence the conditions affecting the security and quality of their lives" (Curnan & Hughes, 2002, p. 33). This approach is exemplified in the Ford Foundation's Community Youth Development Initiative (Cutler & Edwards, 2002), Stanford University's Gardner Center for Youth and Community (McLaughlin, 2000), Annie E. Casey Foundation (Hyman, 1999), Innovation Center for Community & Youth Development at the University of Wisconsin (2002), and the National 4-H Council (2002), to name just a few.

Ultimately, it is the community youth development approach that best embodies the three protective factors of caring relationships, high expectations, and opportunities for participation/contribution. The CYD approach recognizes that youth participation and contribution not only benefit youth themselves, by promoting positive developmental outcomes, but also that youth participation and contribution are critical and necessary if we are to actually improve communities not only for youth, but for everyone. CYD recognizes the web of inter-connectedness that is community, providing a fresh perspective on a familiar adage: "It takes a child to raise a whole village" (Kretzmann & Schmitz, 1999).

A RESILIENT COMMUNITY

A resilient community, like a resilient individual, can be described as having social competence, problem-solving capacity, a sense of identity, and hope for the future. Referred to in the community organization literature as "community capacity" (Chaskin et al., 2001), these characteristics can also be considered the social capital necessary for the health not only of young people but for families and community members as well. A resilient community recognizes the inter-connectedness of all its citizens and understands that the well-being of children and young people is connected to the well-being of other age groups — and vice versa. It is a community in which young people, families, schools, and community members and organizations work in *partnership* with each other to ensure that young people, old people, and all those in between receive the critical supports and opportunities necessary for healthy development throughout the lifespan. A resilient community is characterized by mutually caring relationships, high expectations in the form of shared positive beliefs and respect for all citizens — especially those on the margin (including young people), and by active participation and contribution on the part of everyone.

In a resilient community, community members and organizations support and work in partnership with families, youth, and schools. Families support youth, volunteer in their community, and work in partnership with schools. Schools not only support and work in partnership with their students but also support and work in partnership with families and with community groups, especially with their community-based organization partners. Several prominent successful examples of this approach during the last decade include Families and Schools Together (FAST), developed by Lynn McDonald (McDonald & Moberg, 2000)), the California Wellness Villages described earlier, community schools (Dryfoos, 2003), beacon schools (Walker & Arbreton, 2002), and the less widely known community-wide study circles (Study Circles Resource Center, 2001).

A major finding of almost any successful youth-serving setting or program is that its success was enhanced by creating partnerships with other settings. For example, mentoring by a community organization is more successful when the family is also a partner and when schools are cooperative. After-school programs run by community organizations but located in schools benefit from the commitment of the school and from involved parents. On the other hand, the absence of partnerships and collaboration have the opposite effect.

Likewise, evaluators of the New Futures venture, an ambitious community-wide initiative to benefit young people in five large communities, warn that we neglect the qualities of the immediate caregiving environment — what we have also called social capital — at our peril. Julie White and Gary Wehlage, on-site evaluators of the five-year initiative, which was funded by the Annie E. Casey Foundation, attribute the failure of these early community-wide collaborations to the finding that agencies talked only to each other; they did not, for example, bring in the families or youth they served, nor did they invite teachers to the table. According to White and Wehlage, "It is the strengthening of neighborhoods from the inside that is vital, something that traditional

> **A major finding of almost any successful youth-serving setting or program is that its success was enhanced by creating partnerships with other settings.**

social services have not succeeded in doing" (White & Wehlage, 1995, p. 35). The authors go on to state that if the goal becomes one of "building social capital, the criteria for a successful collaborative would shift from delivering services more efficiently to success in fostering community. Social capital contributes to community by fostering networks of interdependency within and among families, neighborhoods, and the larger community" (p. 35). Furthermore, they argue, "The shift from delivering services to individual clients to investing in the social capital of whole groups of people appears to be essential if collaboratives are to ultimately improve the life chances of generations of at-risk children" (p. 35).

In resilient communities, residents' innate strengths are not only nurtured, they are mobilized — made to bump up against each other and to interact in ways that amplify their effect — to the ultimate benefit of us all.

[*Community Program Protective Factor Indicators* are found in Appendix D.]

CHAPTER 8
A Perspective on Protective Systems

Stepping back from the previous discussion of how families, schools, and communities can promote or prevent the healthy development of young people, what underlying themes — from research and from what young people have told us — should shape our work in the decade ahead?

DEVELOPMENTAL WISDOM

First, just as resilience strengths seem to transcend culture, gender, age, time, and socioeconomic status, so, too, do the protective factors of caring relationships, high expectations, and opportunities to participate and contribute. We hypothesize that the universal power of these three protective factors is their direct relationship to meeting our basic human needs. From a resilience perspective, the capacity for healthy development and successful learning is innate in all people. It is an inborn developmental wisdom that naturally motivates individuals to meet their human needs for love, belonging, respect, identity, mastery, challenge, and meaning.

The youth development process is a direct application of this understanding. When young people experience home, school, and community environments rich in caring relationships, high expectations, and opportunities for meaningful participation and contribution, their developmental needs are met. In turn, having these needs met naturally promotes the individual resilience strengths of social competence, problem-solving skills, autonomy, and sense of purpose and bright future. These individual strengths result in young people's improved social, health, and academic outcomes and protect them from involvement in health-risk behaviors, such as alcohol, tobacco, and other drug abuse; teen pregnancy; and violence (see Figure 6 on next page).

HOW, NOT WHAT

A second key understanding about protective systems is that they do not depend on a particular, "perfect" program. Efforts over the past decade to identify successful research-based approaches have led to numerous meta-analyses of the characteristics of prevention programs (Greenberg et al., 1999;

Tobler et al., 2000), education programs (American Institutes for Research, 1999; American Youth Policy Forum, 1997, 1999), and youth development programs (American Youth Policy Forum, 1997, 1999; Catalano et al., 1999; Eccles & Gootman, 2002). Similarly, in the pages of this document we mention a number of powerful approaches, such as mentoring, service-learning, small schools, and so on. Clearly, some approaches are more promising than others. Yet the major message from long-term studies of human development as well as of successful school and community programs is to realize that programs *per se* are not the answer, it's *how* we do what we do that counts (Benard, 1999).

Figure 6. Youth Development Process: Resiliency in Action

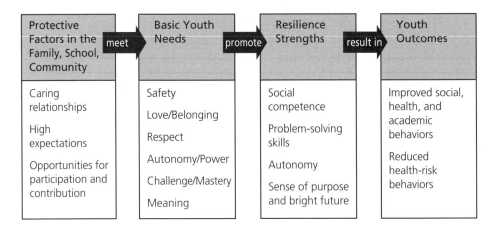

No program design can compensate for a mentor who is not caring, respectful, and reciprocal. A young person's relationship with such a mentor is probably a risk factor and certainly not a protective factor. Likewise, a service-learning project that gives students token roles and rejects them as decision-making partners can actually do harm. It is imperative that practitioners and program evaluation researchers begin to look more at the quality of the program environment, at the climate or ethos of the organization or system in which a program is embedded. The quality of the immediate caregiving environment tells a much more important story than does any particular program approach.

THE POWER OF A SINGLE RELATIONSHIP

A third point is that resilience research confirms unequivocally the power of one person to make a difference. No matter what official role we play in a young person's life (teacher, parent, neighbor, social worker, youthworker, etc.), and no matter for what length of time, we can do it in the caring and empowering ways exemplified by those who become turnaround people for youth. In our relationships with young people, we have the power and responsibility to provide the critical supports and opportunities that build resilience strengths. At the same time, we have the power to undermine those inner characteristics.

At our best, we can honor the incredible developmental wisdom that propels a young person to seek love and belonging, respect, mastery, challenge, and meaning. We can nurture a youth's innate potential for social competence, problem solving, autonomy, and hope — as models ourselves and by guiding a young person to experience these inner qualities within his or her own self. Conversely, we can squander the power of our relationship with a young person. We don't have to be perfect, but we do have to be mindful of our immense power, for good or ill.

"WRAPAROUND" SUPPORT

Finally, while the power of one is real, it is not always enough. Furthermore, the power of more than one — of two, or several, or many — is much more than additive, it is exponential. If we don't want youth falling through the cracks when they leave our family, our classroom, our school, our library, etc., we must work together to weave a fabric of resilience that connects not just young people to their families, schools, and communities but one that connects families to schools and communities, and schools and communities to each other.

Resilience research makes clear that protective factors in one setting have the power to compensate for risks that may be present in other settings. To protect human development, nature and cultures have built in redundancy, allowing for multiple sources of needed support and allowing for responsiveness to such support across the lifespan. As we've seen, children from troubled and non-nurturing families or from dangerous and resource-poor communities have encountered restorative schools and teachers who turned their lives from risk to resilience. Similarly, in the face of dysfunctional and unresponsive schools, youth have found developmental supports and opportunities in their families and in community-based organizations.

> **Resilience research makes clear that protective factors in one setting have the power to compensate for risks that may be present in other settings.**

Given what we know about environmental protections for youth, imagine the possibilities for nurturing the next generation if all of these settings worked together with a shared mission focused on youth development. Imagine further that these collaborations were not only youth-centered but youth-driven, that young people from elementary-school-age on up were partners in the process, that adults asked them what they wanted and needed to be successful and healthy, and that adults worked together with young people to provide these critical supports and opportunities.

Our goal is large, but it is clear. It is to provide the "wraparound" support of youth-driven family-school-community partnerships, partnerships that share a mission of increasing for all young people their experiences of caring relationships, high expectations, and opportunities for participation and contribution.

conclusion

CHAPTER 9

Conclusion

Building on all that has been learned about resilience and youth development, what are the steps ahead? What must we provide for youth and for those who work with them? How can we have the most effect? And what challenges must we address?

BELIEF AND VISION

I suggest that we need to begin with belief in the innate resilience of every human being and with the metaphor that all of us who work with youth are gardeners, whose young people are flowers in our care. Such gardeners understand that, like seeds, children have within them everything they need to be healthy and successful. In our role as gardeners, we do not need to tamper with the seed — the flower is in there. But we must understand the importance of providing a nurturing environment, one that responds to each individual. As a teacher in *The Dreamkeepers: Successful Teachers of African-American Children* observed about her various students, "One might need a little more sunlight, another a little fertilizer. Some might need a little pruning and some might need to roam free" (Ladson-Billings, 1996, p. 89).

If we can focus on our belief in young people's innate resilience and developmental wisdom, we are in a position to find what allows each one to thrive (see Figure 7). Milbrey McLaughlin puts it this way: "The major message we want to get across is that perspective really matters. If adults were to stop viewing young people as something to be fixed and controlled and, instead, helped enable their development, there would be phenomenal change in their lives and society in general" (Portner, 1994, p. 31). Bill Lofquist, the "grandfather" of youth development, takes a similar stance: "If we were to use as a beginning point a new commitment to viewing and respecting young people as resources in all that we do — which, incidentally, would mean that we would also begin viewing and respecting all people as resources — we would create a new basis for shaping a shared vision and clear mission for youth opportunity systems" (1992, p. 23).

Figure 7. When Adults Believe in Resilience

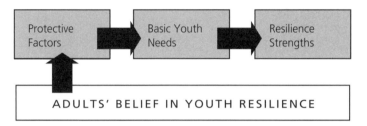

Much progress has been made bringing a strengths perspective to the table. Unfortunately, many human service professions — education, criminal justice, and, even social services — still reflect the deficit model they were founded on. How do we move caregivers with deficit perspectives, and, even more important, how do we transform human service systems so that they take a positive, nurturing approach to human development?

This question is similar to the question that has been at the heart of the resilience movement: How do we transform risk into resilience? One important answer is to help the caregivers of our youth recognize their own resilient nature. Doing so allows them to reframe their experience and see themselves and their lives in new ways. Providing organizational supports and opportunities to the caregivers of youth is a necessary condition for resilience-based youth development. Supporting the "health of the helpers" enhances their ability to live and model resilience strengths — social competence, problem solving, autonomy, and sense of purpose.

Many approaches based on teaching caregivers about their innate resilience are being practiced in a variety of settings. For example, Health Realization (Mills & Spittle, 2001) is used by schools, communities, workplaces, and organizations nationally and internationally to help parents, teachers, managers, youth workers, and law enforcement officers recognize their own resilience so they, in turn, can see the resilience of the populations they serve, including those most challenged. Caregivers who learn about and model their own resilience are also able to directly teach young people about the resilience within themselves and the power they have to see themselves and their lives in new ways. In addition to Mills's work, programs designed by Glenn Richardson (*Resilient Youth Curriculum*) and Steve and Sybil Wolin (*Project Resilience*), among others, fall into this category.

Resilience study groups are common for teaching both caregivers and young people about their personal resilience. Teachers, youth workers, and youth learn about resilience research, read biographies and autobiographies of those who overcame lives of risk, and share their own stories.

The sharing of stories from literature and one's own experience is a powerful reframing strategy for helping people young and old learn about their resilience, the power they each have "to see themselves and their lives in new ways" (O'Gorman, 1994, p. 2). According to Valerie Polakow in her critique of the "at-risk" paradigm, "It is important to read about struggles that lead to empowerment and to successful advocacy, for resilient voices are critical to hear within the at-risk wasteland" (1993, p. 269).

For teachers, learning about resilience experiences and research is critical to closing the achievement gap because it provides evidence and gives hope to educators that all children and youth have the capacity to learn and that teachers and schools actually do have the power to successfully educate them. According to Lisa Delpit, "When teachers…understand that through their teaching change *can* occur, then the chance for transformation is great" (1996, p. 208).

The focus for Dr. Carl Bell, community psychiatrist and trauma expert, is that resilience education reach youth themselves: "When I was in medical school, I was told that if a child came into my office with a rat bite, and I sat in my office, examined the child, and then gave the child a tetanus shot, some antibiotics, and carefully dressed the wound, I would be a good doctor. If, however, 100 children from the surrounding community came into my office, each with rat bites, and I sat in my office, examined the child, and then gave the child a tetanus shot, some antibiotics, carefully dressed the wound, and that was all — then I should have my medical license revoked. The reason being that I did not go out into those children's community and get rid of the rat. In this case, the rat is a lack of vision and leadership to insist that society provide lessons in resiliency [to] our children" (2001, pp. 379–380).

Another approach, reducing the stress of caregivers so that they can see the health in themselves and others is the goal of meditation and mindfulness programs (Kabat-Zinn, 1995). Resilience classes (Vasquez, 2000) and insight meditation (Lozoff, 2000) are becoming more commonplace not only for inmates but also for staff in juvenile halls and prisons — with transformational results. The National Resilience Resource Center at the University of Minnesota is using this health-of-the helper model of change in school districts around the country (Benard & Marshall, 1997; Marshall, 1998).

"When teachers… understand that through their teaching change *can* occur, then the chance for transformation is great."

— Lisa Delpit

Other related approaches include the problem-solving and insight groups advocated by Parker Palmer (1998) in *The Courage to Teach*; reflective practice groups (Schon, 1990), and using a process of "Participation, Observation, Reflection, and Transformation" advocated in *Resilience Education* (Brown et al., 2001). All of these approaches focus on developing the self-awareness and mindfulness that help caregivers get perspective in their work.

Increased research interest is focusing on how giving care from a place of compassion affects the caregiver. "An important direction for future research would be to investigate how support *provision* affects the well-being of the support provider (e.g., mentor).... The well-known helper-therapy principle would suggest that the benefits for the support providers are at least as great as the benefits for the support recipients" (Barrera & Prelow, 2000, p. 333). Instead of burning out or developing compassion fatigue, caregivers with a resilient attitude — belief in their own innate capacity as well as in the capacities of their young people — may instead be protected by feelings of self-efficacy, optimism, and hope — for themselves and their young people. As one special education teacher explains, "People often ask me whether I am 'drained' by working with so many needy, troubled kids, day in and day out. My answer is no! My life will forever be changed for the better because of these courageous survivors. I will be watching them as their hearts warm and their souls mend further.... I will shout their resilience from the mountain tops!" (L. Bell, 1998, p. 26).

Finally, much research from the medical field, including brain science but especially in the area of mind-body, stress, and psycho-neuro-immunology research (H. Benson, 1996; Dossey, 2003; Kabat-Zinn, 1995; Ornstein & Sobel, 1987; Pert, 1997), has clearly established humankind's innate self-righting, resilient nature and points to the additional power of our thoughts and beliefs to promote healing. While seldom integrated into the resilience/assets/youth development literature, these lines of scientific research provide great promise to inform and support social scientists, parents, educators, youth workers, advocates, and even systems working with resilience and youth development approaches.

CHALLENGES AHEAD

This document concludes with challenges, which, according to resilience practice, are viewed as opportunities, not as problems. The first challenge is to the research, funding, and policy commutities to focus more time and resources on the study of resilience. "Our choices about what to research and how to go about it are conditioned by where we hope to go in the broadest sense. Our ideas about values, aesthetics, politics, and normal behavior and preferences are integral to educational research, its interpretation, and its utilization. Science and research cannot determine or validate these values, visions, and ideas. Science and research can only be used to help us develop effective methods for working toward our values, visions, and ideas" (Shannon, 1995, p. 127).

A second challenge is to practitioners and caregivers, to believe in their own innate resilience, to understand it so that they can model it and see it within their young people. The "power of one" is clearly a major finding of four decades of resilience research, validating the influence each of us has in every interaction with children and young people — to nurture or block — their innate resilience.

A second challenge is to practitioners and caregivers, to believe in their own innate resilience, to understand it so that they can model it and see it within their young people.

Yet as important as our individual relationships with young people are, they are not enough, especially in the face of the barriers to change within some human services and education bureaucracies. So the third challenge is to our youth-serving systems and bureaucracies. As Lisbeth Schorr found when analyzing why half of the successful programs for children and families that she had reported on in *Within Our Reach* (1988) were defunct five years later and none had been expanded or replicated, she concluded in her subsequent book, *Common Purpose* (1997), that "When effective programs aiming to reach large numbers encounter the pressures exercised by prevailing attitudes and systems, the resulting collision is almost always lethal to the effective programs. Their demise can be prevented only by changing systems and public perceptions to make them more hospitable to effective efforts to change lives and communities" (p. 20). McLaughlin (2000), as well as the Institute of Medicine, comes to the same conclusion in discussing the challenges to sustaining community youth-serving organizations.

According to the Institute of Medicine report, "Both quantitative and qualitative implementation data also tell us a great deal about why programs fail. These studies make it clear how the programs are nested into larger social systems that need to be taken into account. When adequate supports are not available in these larger systems, it is unlikely that specific programs will be able to be implemented well and sustained over time" (Eccles & Gootman, 2002, p. 221).

Schorr's great hope is that we begin to move bureaucracies and systems to make large-scale system changes in support of the local wisdom and strengths

The third challenge
is to our youth-
serving systems and
bureaucracies, to make
large-scale system
changes in support of
the local wisdom and
strengths represented in
successful programs.

represented in successful programs — without insisting that what works in one community must necessarily work in another. She hopes that while these service systems would be oriented toward building social capital, they would also "find ways to surmount obstacles to fundamental systems change so that the *attributes* [emphasis added] of successful demonstrations [or efforts] can become the norms of mainstream systems" (1997, p. 381).

A decade ago only the most skeptical would have foreseen that as the 21st century rolls on, Americans still do not have universal access to programs like Head Start and Early Head Start, health care, after-school programs, family support efforts, comprehensive school health programs, full-service schools, job training, alternative degree programs, and so on. Schorr's call for a human agenda in which "every American family can expect its children to grow up with hope in their hearts and a realistic expectation that they will participate in the American dream" (1997, p. 385) remains only a vision.

It is the "business of us all," Harold Howe proposes in the closing chapter of *The Forgotten Half Revisited*, a report published by the American Youth Policy Forum (Halperin, 1998), to start where we are — here in the moment, ourselves — to build social capital for children, youth, and families in this new century. Howe summarizes the report as an attempt "to capture the qualities of hope, fortitude and the essential importance of working at improving human relationships across the boundaries of economic status and other barriers. The [report's] recommendations speak of caring adult-youth relationships, the demands of family life, community-based activities, service opportunities and other such concepts. All these elements demand a quality of caring for each other that cannot be measured. Neither can it be legislated. Its presence among us is the business of all of us" (p. 178).

Fortunately, the caring that Howe calls for is inherent in each of us. It is one of the most necessary and powerful of the resilience strengths we humans are born with. Our "business," as Howe says, is to use it.

Matrix of Personal Strengths

Resilience (Benard)[1]	Social Competence	Problem Solving	Autonomy	Purpose/Future	Others
Resilience (Wolin)[2]	Relationships	Insight	Independence, Initiative, Humor	Creativity, Morality	
Maslow[3]	Need for Love/ Belonging	Need for Challenge & Mastery	Need for Power, Respect	Need for Meaning	Need for Safety
Postive Psychology VIA Strengths[4]	Humanity (Kindness/ Loving)	Wisdom	Temperance, Self-Control	Transcendence, Courage, Perseverance	Justice & Wisdom
Emotional Intelligence (Goleman)[5]	Empathy, Handling Relationships	Problem Solving	Self-Awareness, Emotional Control	Self-Motivation	
Kumpfer (1999)[6]	Social/Behavioral	Cognitive	Emotional Management	Spiritual	Physical Well-Being
Search Institute of Internal Assets[7]	Social Competence, Positive Values	Social Competence	Positive Identity	Commitment to Learning	
Youth Development (Pittman)[8]	Social	Intellectual, Cognitive/Mental	Emotional, Conflict Resolution, Self-Regulating, Coping	Spiritual	Physical
Institute of Medicine/Youth Development[9]	Connectedness, Cultural Competence	Planfulness	Efficacy, Autonomy, Initiative	Civic Engagement, Optimism, Mastery & Achievement	Good Health Habits
Multiple Intelligences (Gardner)[10]	Interpersonal	Logical-Mathematical, Linguistic	Intrapersonal	Intrapersonal, Existential	Musical, Spatial, Bodily-Kinesthetic, Naturalist
Erikson's Development Stages[11]	Trust, Cool, Generosity	Industry	Identity, Autonomy, Initiative	Integrity	
Vaillant (2002)[12]	Empathy, Sociability, Gratitude, Forgiveness	Planning		Future Orientation, Optimism	
SCANS Report [13]	Sociability, Listening, Speaking	Reasoning, Problem Solving, Creative Thinking, Decision-Making, Metacognition	Self-Management, Self-Esteem	Responsibility	Integrity/Honesty, Reading, Writing, Mathematics
Durlak [14]	Social	Academic	Psychological	Psychological	Physical
Megaskills (Rich)[15]	Caring, Teamwork	Common Sense, Problem Solving	Effort, Confidence, Initiative	Motivation, Responsibility, Perseverance	Focus
Strayhorn (1988)[16]	Empathy, Trust, Social Skills	Frustration Tolerance, Exploration, Discovery, Problem Solving	Independence, Self-Awareness	Meaning	

FOOTNOTES FOR APPENDIX A: MATRIX OF PERSONAL STRENGTHS

1   Benard, B. (1991). *Fostering resiliency in kids: Protective factors in the family, school, and community.* Portland, OR: Northwest Regional Educational Laboratory.

2   Wolin, S. & Wolin, S. (1993). *The resilient self: How survivors of troubled families rise above adversity.* New York: Villard Books.

3   Maslow, A. (1954). *Motivation and personality.* New York: Harper and Row.

4   Peterson, C. & Seligman, M. (2003). *Values in action classification of strengths.* Retrieved from http://www.positivepsychology.org/taxonomy.htm

5   Goleman, D. (1995). *Emotional intelligence. Why it can matter more than I.Q.* New York: Bantam Books.

6   Kumpfer, K. (1999). Factors and processes contributing to resilience: The resilience framework. In M. Glantz & J. Johnson (Eds.), *Resilience and development: Positive life adaptations* (pp. 269–277). New York: Kluwer.

7   Benson, P. (1997). *All kids are our kids: What communities must do to raise caring and responsible children and adolescents.* San Francisco: Jossey-Bass.

8   Pittman, K. & Zeldin, S. (1995). *Premises, principles, and practices: Defining the why, what, and how of promoting youth development through organizational practice.* Washington, DC: Academy for Educational Development, Center for Youth Development & Policy Research.

9   Eccles, J. & Gootman, J. (2002). *Community programs to promote youth development.* Washington, DC: National Academies Press.

10 Gardner, H. (1993). *Multiple intelligences: The theory in practice.* New York: Basic Books.

11 Erickson, E. (1963). *Childhood and society.* New York: W. W. Norton.

12 Vaillant, G. (2002). *Aging well: Surprising guideposts to a happier life from the landmark Harvard study of adult development.* Boston: Little, Brown and Company.

13 Secretary's Commission on Achieving Necessary Skills (SCANS) Report, U.S. Department of Labor. (2000). *Learning a living: A blueprint for high performance.* Baltimore: The Johns Hopkins University Institute for Policy Studies. Retrieved from http://wdr.doleta.gov/SCANS/lal/LAL.HTM

14 Durlak, J. (2000). Health promotion as a strategy in primary prevention. In D. Cicchetti, J. Rappaport, I. Sandler, & R. Weissberg (Eds.), *The promotion of wellness in children and adolescents* (pp. 221–241). Washington, DC: Child Welfare League Association Press.

15 Rich, D. (1998). *MegaSkills: Building children's achievement for the information age.* New York: Houghton-Mifflin.

16 Strayhorn, J. (1988). *The competent child: An approach to psychotherapy and preventive mental health.* New York: Guilford.

Family Protective Factor Indicators

FAMILY: CARING AND SUPPORT

Models and teaches empathy and compassion
Aims to meet developmental needs for belonging and connection
Is available/responsive/trustworthy
Creates one-to-one time
Actively listens
Models "I" messages/assertive communication skills
Shows common courtesy
Shows respect
Is warm and affectionate
Uses loving touch
Pays personalized attention
Shows interest
Checks in often
Gets to know hopes and dreams
Shows respect for and acknowledges child's feelings
Names and accepts feelings
Communicates unconditional love
Accepts child for who s/he is — not what parent wants him/her to be
Looks beneath "problem" behavior
Reaches beyond the resistance
Laughs, plays, smiles, and uses humor
Shows patience
Has fun with
Encourages connections to other caring adults
Helps create a sense of belonging to culture
Relates to child's teacher/school with empathy and partnership
Creates connections to other supportive community resources:
    Cultural
    Educational
    Recreational
    Religious/spiritual
    Health care
    Counseling and social services

FAMILY: HIGH EXPECTATIONS

Believes in and teaches innate resilience ("You have what it takes," "You can rise above this," "You have a power within you," etc.)

Believes in innate capacity of child to be successful

Models and teaches that mistakes and setbacks are opportunities for growth

Helps child understand what s/he can and cannot control

Models and teaches adaptive distancing skills

Helps to reframe problems into opportunities

Models and teaches critical thinking, critical consciousness

Encourages self-awareness of moods and thinking

Challenges and supports ("You can do it," "I'll be there to help.")

Conveys "no excuses, never give up" philosophy (persistence/determination)

Aims to meet developmental needs for mastery, challenge, and meaning

Conveys to child that s/he has gifts to "give back" to the community

Focuses on meeting needs of whole child (social, emotional, cognitive, physical, spiritual)

Encourages creativity and imagination

Conveys optimism and hope

Accepts child for who s/he is — not what family member wants her or him to be

Honors the unique gifts of each child ("There has never been another *you*.")

Recognizes strengths and special interests

Mirrors strengths and special interests

Affirms/encourages strengths and interests

Uses strengths and interests to address concerns/problems

Provides success experiences that build on child's interests, strengths, dreams, and goals

Helps teachers and others see child's strengths, interests, and goals

Advocates for child at school and elsewhere

Understands the needs motivating child's behavior

Does not take child's behavior personally

Attributes the best possible motive to behavior

Models high standards for behavior

Articulates clear expectations/boundaries/structure

Knows child's friends

Knows child's whereabouts

Rules and discipline are consistent but fair and flexible

Uses positive feedback and encouragement

Provides clear explanations

Chooses battles

Holds child accountable with natural consequences (not arbitrary punishment)

Models boundary-setting

Uses family and cultural rituals and traditions

Shares family and cultural stories

Models and teaches "accommodation without assimilation"

Continuously challenges racism, sexism, ageism, classism, and homophobia

FAMILY: PARTICIPATION/CONTRIBUTION

Aims to meet developmental needs for power/autonomy and meaning
Gives meaningful responsibilities
Divides up family chores fairly
Models and provides opportunities for planning
Models and provides opportunities for decision-making
Models and provides opportunities for problem solving
Gives child voice in creating rules and discipline
Gives child opportunity to make amends for mistakes and misbehavior
Holds regular family meetings
Makes time for personal reflection and dialog/discussion
Provides opportunities for child to help others in home, school, or community
Creates opportunities for creative expression
      Art
      Music
      Writing/Poetry
      Storytelling/Drama
Provides opportunities for child to develop, use, and contribute his or her
      Strengths and interests
      Goals and dreams
Provides opportunities for child to be part of
      Adventure/outdoor experience programs
      Community service programs
      Peer helping, cross-age helping
      Peer support and other small-group processes
      Cooperative learning
      Small, interest-based groups
Sees that child's after-school program has a youth development (not just academic) focus

School Protective Factor Indicators

SCHOOL: CARING AND SUPPORT

Creates and sustains a caring climate
Models empathy and compassion
Aims to meet developmental needs for belonging and respect
Is available/responsive
Offers extra individualized help
Has long-term commitment
Creates one-to-one time
Actively listens/gives voice
Shows common courtesy
Respects others
Uses appropriate self-disclosure
Pays personalized attention
Shows interest
Checks in
Gets to know hopes and dreams
Gets to know life context
Gets to know interests
Shows respect for and acknowledges student's feelings
Names and accepts student's feelings
Provides fundamental positive regard
Is nonjudgmental
Looks beneath "problem" behavior
Reaches beyond the resistance
Uses humor/smiles/laughter
Is flexible
Shows patience
Uses community-building process
Creates small, personalized groups
Creates opportunities for peer helping
Uses cross-age mentors (older students, family/community members)
Creates connections to resources:
     Education
     Cultural
     Employment
     Recreation
     Health, counseling, and social services

SCHOOL: HIGH EXPECTATIONS

Sustains a high expectation climate honoring each student's unique strengths
Conveys "no excuses, never give up" philosophy (persistence/determination)
Models and teaches that mistakes and setbacks are opportunities for learning
Aims to meet developmental needs for mastery, challenge, and meaning
Believes in innate capacity of all to learn
Sees students as vital partners in school improvement
Focuses on whole child (social, emotional, cognitive, physical, spiritual)
Understands the needs motivating student behavior and learning
Sees culture as an asset
Challenges and supports ("You can do it," "I'll be there to help.")
Connects learning to students' interests, strengths, experiences, dreams, and goals
Encourages creativity and imagination
Conveys optimism and hope
Affirms/encourages the best in students
Attributes the best possible motive to behavior
Articulates clear expectations/boundaries/structure
Provides clear explanations
Holds students accountable
Models boundary-setting
Uses discipline that is consistent, strict, and fair
Models and teaches adaptive distancing and conflict resolution
Uses rituals and traditions
Recognizes strengths and interests
Mirrors strengths and interests
Uses strengths and interests to address concerns/problems
Uses a variety of instructional strategies to tap multiple intelligences
Employs authentic assessment
Groups students heterogeneously
Continuously challenges racism, sexism, ageism, classism, and homophobia
Helps to reframe self-image from at-risk to at-promise
Helps to reframe problems into opportunities
Conveys message to students that they are resilient
Sees students as constructors of own knowledge and meaning
Teaches critical analysis/consciousness
Encourages self-awareness of moods and thinking
Relates to family and community members with high expectations
Calls home to report students' good behavior and achievements
Helps family members see students' strengths, interests, and goals

SCHOOL: PARTICIPATION/CONTRIBUTION

Builds a democratic, inclusive community
Practices equity and inclusion
Aims to meet developmental needs for power/autonomy and meaning
Provides opportunities for planning
Provides opportunities for decision-making
Provides opportunities for problem solving
Empowers students to create classroom rules
Holds regular and as-needed class meetings
Gives youth meaningful roles and responsibilities
Infuses communication skills into all learning experiences
 Reading
 Writing
 Relationship
 Cross-cultural
Creates opportunities for creative expression
 Art
 Music
 Writing/Poetry
 Storytelling/Drama
Provides opportunities for students to use/contribute their
 Strengths and interests
 Goals and dreams
Includes and engages marginalized groups
 Girls/Women
 Students of color
 Students with special needs
Infuses service/active learning
Uses adventure/outdoor experience-based learning
Offers community service
Offers peer helping
Offers cross-age helping
Offers peer-support groups
Uses cooperative learning
Provides ongoing opportunities for personal reflection
Provides ongoing opportunities for dialog/discussion
Uses small, interest-based groups
Uses group processes/cooperative learning
Uses restorative justice circles in place of punitive discipline
Engages students — especially those on the margin — in a school climate improvement task force
Invites the participation and contribution of family and community members in meaningful classroom activities (not just cookie-baking)

Community Program Protective Factor Indicators

COMMUNITY: CARING AND SUPPORT

Creates and sustains a caring climate
Models empathy and compassion
Aims to meet developmental needs for belonging and respect
Is available/responsive
Offers extra individualized help
Has long-term commitment
Creates one-to-one time
Actively listens/gives voice
Shows common courtesy
Respects young people
Uses appropriate self-disclosure
Pays personalized attention
Shows interest
Checks in
Gets to know hopes and dreams of youth
Gets to know life context
Gets to know interests
Shows respect for and acknowledges young people's feelings
Names and accepts young people's feelings
Conveys fundamental positive regard
Is nonjudgmental
Looks beneath "problem" behavior
Reaches beyond the resistance
Uses humor/smiles/laughter
Is flexible
Shows patience
Uses community-building process
Creates small, personalized groups
Creates opportunities for peer-helping
Uses cross-age mentors (older youth, family/community members)
Creates connections to resources:
    Education
    Culture
    Employment
    Recreation
    Health care, counseling, and social services

COMMUNITY: HIGH EXPECTATIONS

Sustains a high expectation climate honoring each youth's unique strengths

Conveys a "no excuses, never give up" philosophy (persistence/determination)

Models and teaches that mistakes and setbacks are opportunities for growth

Aims to meet developmental needs for mastery, challenge, and meaning

Believes that young people are a community resource

Sees youth as vital partners in improving community

Focuses on meeting needs of whole child (social, emotional, cognitive, physical, spiritual)

Understands the needs motivating young people's behavior and learning

Sees culture as an asset

Challenges and supports ("You can do it," "I'll be there to help.")

Connects learning to students' interests, strengths, experiences, dreams, and goals

Encourages creativity and imagination

Conveys optimism and hope

Affirms/encourages the best in youth

Attributes the best possible motive to behavior

Articulates clear expectations/boundaries/structure

Uses discipline that is consistent, strict, and fair

Provides clear explanations

Holds young people accountable

Models boundary-setting

Models and teaches adaptive distancing and conflict resolution

Uses rituals and traditions

Recognizes strengths and interests of youth

Mirrors strengths and interests

Uses strengths and interests to address concerns/problems

Uses a variety of instructional strategies to tap multiple intelligences

Groups youth heterogeneously

Continuously challenges racism, sexism, ageism, classism, and homophobia

Helps to reframe self-image from at-risk to at-promise

Helps to reframe problems into opportunities

Conveys message to youth that they are resilient

Sees youth as constructors of own knowledge and meaning

Teaches critical analysis/consciousness

Encourages self-awareness of moods and thinking

Relates to family, school, and other community members with high expectations

Calls home and school to report youth's good behavior and achievements

Helps family and school recognize youth's strengths, interests, and goals

COMMUNITY: PARTICIPATION/CONTRIBUTION

Builds a democratic, inclusive community
Practices equity and inclusion
Aims to meet developmental needs for power/autonomy and meaning
Provides opportunities for planning
Provides opportunities for decision-making
Provides opportunities for problem solving
Empowers youth to help create organization's rules
Holds regular and as-needed organizational meetings of all youth
Gives youth meaningful roles and responsibilities
Infuses communication skills into all learning experiences
    Reading
    Writing
    Relationship
    Cross-cultural
Creates opportunities for creative expression
    Art
    Music
    Writing/Poetry
    Storytelling/Drama
Provides opportunities for youth to use/contribute their
    Strengths and interests
    Goals and dreams
Includes and engages marginalized groups
    Girls/Women
    Youth of color
    Youth with special needs
Provides opportunities for community service/active learning
Provides opportunities for adventure/outdoor experiences
Provides opportunities for peer helping
Provides opportunities for cross-age helping
Provides peer-support groups
Provides ongoing opportunities for personal reflection
Provides ongoing opportunities for dialog/discussion
Uses small, interest-based groups
Uses group processes/cooperative learning
Uses restorative justice circles in place of punitive discipline
Engages students — especially those on the margin — in a program/organization/community improvement task force
Creates collaborative partnerships with youth, family, school, and other community members

References

Adams, G., Bullotta, T., & Montemayor, R. (Eds.). (1992). *Adolescent identity formation.* Newbury Park, CA: Sage.

American Institutes for Research. (1999). *An educator's guide to schoolwide reform.* Arlington, VA: Author.

American Youth Policy Forum. (1997, 1999). *Some things DO make a difference for youth: A compendium of evaluations of youth programs and practices, Volumes I and II.* Washington, DC: Institute for Educational Leadership.

Anderman, E., Austin, C., & Johnson D. (2002). The development of goal orientation. In A. Wigfield & J. Eccles (Eds.), *Development of achievement motivation* (pp. 197–220). New York: Academic Press.

The Annie E. Casey Foundation. *PRB/KIDS COUNT special report: A first look at Census 2000 supplementary survey data* (p. 24). Retrieved from http://www.aecf.org/kidscount/c2ss/pdfs/front/national_profile.pdf

Anthony, E. J. (1974). The syndrome of the psychological invulnerable child. In E.J. Anthony (Ed.), *The child in his family, Vol. 3: Children at psychiatric risk* (pp. 529–544). New York: John Wiley and Sons.

Aronson, E. (2000). *Nobody left to hate: Teaching compassion after Columbine.* New York: Worth Publishers.

August, D. & Hakuta, K. (Eds.). (1997). *Improving schooling for language-minority children: A research agenda.* Washington, DC: National Academies Press.

Averill, J. (2002). Emotional creativity: Toward "spiritualizing the passions." In C. Snyder & S. Lopez (Eds.), *Handbook of positive psychology* (pp. 172–185). New York: Oxford University Press.

Ayers, W. & Ford, P. (Eds.). (1996). *City kids, city teachers: Reports from the front row.* New York: The New Press.

Bacon, J. (1995). The place for life and learning: National Teacher of the Year, Sandra McBrayer. *Journal of Emotional and Behavioral Problems, 3* (4), 42–45.

Baldwin, J. (2001, Spring). Tales of the urban high school. *Carnegie Reporter,* 23–29.

Baldwin, A., Baldwin, C., Kasser, T., Zax, M., Sameroff, A., & Seifer, R. (1993). Contextual risk and resiliency during late adolescence. *Development and Psychopathology, 5,* 743–761.

Bandura, A. (Ed.). (1995). *Self-efficacy in changing societies.* Cambridge, UK: Cambridge University Press.

Bandura, A. (1997). *Self-efficacy: The exercise of control.* New York: W.H. Freeman.

Barber, B. (1996). Parental psychological control: Revisiting a neglected construct. *Child Development, 67,* 3296–3319.

Barber, B. (1997). Introduction to special issue: Adolescent socialization in context — The role of connection, regulation, and autonomy in the family. *Journal of Adolescent Research, 12,* 5–11.

Barber, B. (Ed.). (2002). *Intrusive parenting: How psychological control affects children and adolescents.* New York: American Psychological Association.

Barber, B. & Harmon, E. (2002). Violating the self: Parental psychological control of children and adolescents. In B. Barber (Ed.), *Intrusive parenting: How psychological control affects children and adolescents* (pp. 15–22). New York: American Psychological Association.

Barber, B. & Olsen, J. (1997). Socialization in context: Connection, regulation, and autonomy in the family, school, and neighborhood, and with peers. *Journal of Adolescent Research, 12,* 287–315.

Barrera, M. & Prelow, H. (2000). Interventions to promote social support in children and adolescents. In D. Cicchetti, J. Rappaport, I. Sandler, & R. Weissberg (Eds.), *The promotion of wellness in children and adolescents* (pp. 309–339). Washington, DC: Child Welfare League Association Press.

Batson, C., Ahmad, N., Lishner, D., & Tsang, J. (2002). Empathy and altruism. In C. Snyder & S. Lopez (Eds.), *Handbook of positive psychology* (pp. 485–498). New York: Oxford University Press.

Battistich, V. (2001, April). Effects of an elementary school intervention on students' "connectedness to school and social adjustment during middle school. In J. Brown (Chair), *Resilience education: Theoretical, interactive and empirical applications*. Symposium conducted at the annual meeting of the American Educational Research Association, Seattle.

Battistich, V., Schaps, E., Watson, M., & Solomon, D. (1995). Prevention effects of the Child Development Project: Early findings from an ongoing multisite demonstration trail. *Journal of Adolescent Research, 11,* 12–35.

Battistich, V., Solomon, D., Watson, M., & Schaps, E. (1997). Caring school communities. *Educational Psychologist, 32,* 137–151.

Baumeister, R. (1991). *Meanings of life.* New York: Guilford.

Baumeister, R. & Leary, M. (1995). The need to belong: Desire for interpersonal attachments as a fundamental human motivation. *Psychological Bulletin, 117,* 497–529.

Baumeister, R. & Vohs, K. (2002). The pursuit of meaningfulness in life. In C. Snyder & S. Lopez (Eds.), *Handbook of positive psychology* (pp. 608–618). New York: Oxford University Press.

Beardslee, W. (1997). Prevention and the clinical encounter. *American Journal of Orthopsychiatry, 68,* 521–533.

Beardslee, W. & Podoresfky, D. (1988). Resilient adolescents whose parents have serious affective and other psychiatric disorders: The importance of self-understanding and relationships. *American Journal of Psychiatry, 145,* 63–69.

Bearman, P., Bruckner, H., Brown, B., Tehobald, W., & Philliber, S. (1999). *Peer potential: Making the most of how teens influence each other.* Washington, DC: National Campaign to Prevent Teen Pregnancy.

Beauvais, F. & Oetting, E. (1999). Drug use, resilience, and the myth of the golden child. In M. Glantz & J. Johnson (Eds.), *Resilience and development: Positive life adaptations* (pp. 101–107). New York: Kluwer.

Bell, C. (2001). Cultivating resiliency in youth. *Journal of Adolescent Health, 29,* 375–381.

Bell, L. (1998). Experiencing professional renewal through nurturing young survivors. *Reaching Today's Youth: The Community Circle of Caring Journal, 2*(3), 24–26.

Bellah, R. (1992). *The good society.* New York: Vintage.

Benard, B. (1991). *Fostering resiliency in kids: Protective factors in the family, school, and community.* Portland, OR: Northwest Regional Educational Laboratory.

Benard, B. (1996). Fostering resiliency in urban schools. In B. Williams (Ed.), *Closing the achievement gap: A vision for changing beliefs and practice* (pp. 96–119). Alexandria, VA: Association for Supervision and Curriculum Development.

Benard, B. (1997, Spring). Focusing therapy on what families do right: An interview with Steven Wolin. *Resiliency in Action,* 17–21.

Benard, B. (1999). Applications of resilience In M. Glantz & J. Johnson (Eds.), *Resilience and development: Positive life adaptations* (pp. 269–277). New York: Kluwer.

Benard, B. (2002). Turnaround people and places: Moving from risk to resilience. In D. Saleebey (Ed.), *The strengths perspective in social work practice* (3rd. ed., pp. 213–227). Boston, MA: Allyn Bacon.

Benard, B. (2003). Turnaround teachers and schools. In B. Williams (Ed.), *Closing the Achievement Gap* (2nd ed.). Alexandria, VA: Association for Supervision and Curriculum Development.

Benard, B. & Marshall, K. (1997). A framework for practice: Tapping innate resilience. *Research/Practice: A publication from the Center for Applied Research and Educational Improvement.* (College of Education & Human Development, University of Minnesota), *5*(1), 9–15.

Beneke, T. (1997). Triumph of the heart: An interview with Lillian Rubin. *East Bay Express, 19*(22), 7–15.

Bennett-Goleman, T. (2001). *Emotional alchemy: How the mind can heal the heart.* New York: Harmony Books.

Bennis, W. (1994). *On becoming a leader* (2nd ed.). New York: Perseus.

Bensman, D. (1994). *Lives of the graduates of Central Park East Elementary School: Where have they gone? What did they really learn?* New York: National Center for Restructuring Education, Schools, and Teaching, Teachers College.

Benson, H. (1996). *Timeless healing: The power and biology of belief.* New York: Scribner's.

Benson, P. (1997). *All kids are our kids: What communities must do to raise caring and responsible children and adolescents.* San Francisco: Jossey-Bass.

Benson, P., Masters, K., & Larson, D. (1997). Religious influences on child and adolescent development. In J. Noshpitz & N. Alessi (Eds.), *Handbook of child and adolescent psychiatry: Vol. 4. Varieties of development* (pp. 206–219). New York: John Wiley and Sons.

Bilchik, S. (1998). *Guide for implementing the balanced and restorative justice model.* Rockville, MD: Department of Justice, Office of Juvenile Justice and Delinquency Prevention.

Black, M. & Krishnakumar, A. (1998). Children in low-income, urban settings: Interventions to promote mental health and well-being. *American Psychologist, 53,* 635–646.

Blakeslee, S. & Wallerstein, J. (1989). *Second chances: Men, women and children a decade after divorce.* Boston: Ticknor and Fields.

Blum, R., Beuhring, T., & Rinehart, P. (2000). *Protecting teens: Beyond race, income, and family structure.* Minneapolis: University of Minnesota: Center for Adolescent Health.

Blum, R., Beuhring, T., Shew, M., Bearinger, L., Sieving, R., & Resnick, M. (2000). The effects of race/ethnicity, income, and family structure on adolescent risk behaviors. *American Journal of Public Health, 90,* 1879–1884.

Blum, R. & McNeely, C. (2002). *Improving the odds: The untapped power of schools to improve the health of teens.* Minneapolis, MN: University of Minnesota, Center for Adolescent Health and Development.

Blyth, D. (1993). *Healthy communities, healthy youth: How communities contribute to positive youth development.* Minneapolis, MN: Search Institute.

Blyth, D. & Leffert, N. (1995). Communities as contexts for adolescent development: An empirical analysis. *Journal of Adolescent Research, 3,* 64–87.

Blyth, D. & Roehlkepartain, E. (1993). *Healthy communities, healthy youth.* Minneapolis, MN: Search Institute.

Bosworth, K. & Earthman, E. (2002). From theory to practice: School leaders' perspectives on resiliency. *Journal of Clinical Psychology, 58,* 299–306.

Boykin, K. & Allen, J. (2001). Autonomy and adolescent social functioning: The moderating effect of risk. *Child Development, 72,* 220–235.

Bronfenbrenner, U. (1974). *The ecology of human development.* Cambridge, MA: Harvard University Press.

Brooks, R. & Goldstein, S. (2001). *Raising resilient children: Fostering strength, hope, and optimism in your child.* New York: McGraw-Hill/Contemporary Books.

Brown, G. (1990). *Human teaching for human learning: An introduction to confluent education* (original work published 1972). Highland, NY: Gestalt Journal.

Brown J. & D'Emidio-Caston, M. (1995). On becoming at-risk through drug education: How symbolic policies and their practices affect students. *Evaluation Review, 19* (4), 451–492.

Brown, J., D'Emidio-Caston, M., & Benard, B. (2001). *Resilience education.* Thousand Oaks, CA: Corwin Press.

Brownlee, S. (1996, November 11). Invincible kids. *U.S. News & World Report,* 62–71.

Bruer, J. (1999). *The myth of the first three years.* New York: The Free Press.

Burger, J. (1995). Lightness of being: The value of humor for health, healing, and recovery. *Reclaiming Children and Youth, 4*(3), 13–15.

Butler, K. (1997, March/April). The anatomy of resilience. *Networker,* 22–31.

Carnegie Task Force on Education of Young Adolescents. (1989). *Turning points: Preparing American youth for the 21ˢᵗ century.* New York: Carnegie Corporation.

Carnegie Task Force on Youth Development and Community Programs. (1992). *A matter of time: Risk and opportunity in the nonschool hours.* New York: Carnegie Corporation.

Carver, C. & Scheier, M. (2002). Optimism. In C. Snyder & S. Lopez (Eds.), *Handbook of positive psychology* (pp. 231–243). New York: Oxford University Press.

Cassell, E. (2002). Compassion. In C. Snyder & S. Lopez (Eds.), *Handbook of positive psychology* (pp. 434–445). New York: Oxford University Press.

Catalano, R., Berglund, M., Ryan, J., Lonczak, H., & Hawkins, J. (1999). Positive youth development in the United States: Research findings on evaluations of positive youth development programs. Seattle: Social Development Research Group, University of Washington.

Catterall, J. (1997). Involvement in the arts and success in secondary school. *Americans for the Arts Monographs, 1*(9).

Center for the Study and Prevention of Violence. (n.d.). *Blueprints for violence prevention: Model programs/ promising programs.* University of Colorado. Retrieved from University of Colorado, Center for the Study and Prevention and Violence Web sites. Retrieved from http://www.colorado.edu/cspv/blueprints/model/overview.html and http://www.colorado.edu/cspv/blueprints/promising/overview.html

Cervone, B. (2002). Common ground: Young people harvest food and community. *CYD Journal, 3*(1), 9–15.

Chalk, R. & Phillips, D. (Eds.). (1996). *Youth development and neighborhood influences: Summary of a workshop.* Washington, DC: National Academies Press.

Chao, R. (1994). Beyond parental control and authoritarian parenting style: Understanding Chinese parenting through the cultural notion of training. *Child Development, 65,* 1111–1119.

Chao, R. (2001). Extending research on the consequences of parenting style for Chinese Americans and European Americans. *Child Development, 72,* 1832–1843.

Chaskin, R., Brown, P., Venkatesh, S., & Vidal, A. (2001). *Building community capacity.* New York: Walter de Gruyter.

Chess, S. (1989). Defying the voice of doom. In T. Dugan & R. Coles (Eds.), *The child in our time: Studies in the development of resiliency* (pp. 179–199). New York: Bruner/Mazel.

Children's Express. (1993). *Voices from the future: Children tell us about violence in America.* New York: Crown.

Chirkov, V. & Ryan, R. (2001). Parent and teacher autonomy-support in Russian and U.S. adolescents: Common effects on well-being and academic motivation. *Journal of Cross-Cultural Psychology, 32,* 618–635.

Cicchetti, D., Rappaport, J., Sandler, I., & Weissberg, R. (Eds.). *The promotion of wellness in children and adolescents* (pp. 133–184). Washington, DC: Child Welfare League of America.

Clark, R. (1984). *Family life and school achievement: Why poor black children succeed or fail.* Chicago: University of Chicago Press.

Clausen, J. (1993). *American lives: Looking back at the children of the great depression.* New York: Free Press.

Cleland, R., Jemmott, F., & Angeles, F. (2001). Helping ourselves to health: Youth lead Wellness Villages in California. *CYD Journal, 2*(1), 7–13. Retrieved from http://www.cydjournal.org/2001Winter/contents.html

Cohen, E. (1994). *Designing groupwork: Strategies for the heterogeneous classroom* (2nd ed.). New York: Teachers College Press.

Cohn, J. (1997). *Raising compassionate, courageous children in a violent world.* Atlanta, GA: Longstreet Press.

Coles, R. (1986). *The moral life of children.* Boston: Houghton Mifflin.

Coles, R. (1990). *The spiritual life of children.* Boston: Houghton Mifflin.

Comer, J., Haynes, N., Joyner, E., & Ben-Avie, M. (Eds.). (1996). *Rallying the whole village: The comer process for reforming education.* New York: Teachers College Press.

Connell, J., Kubisch, A., Schorr, L., & Weiss, L. (Eds.). (1995). *New approaches to evaluating community initiatives: Concepts, methods, and contexts.* Washington, DC: Aspen Institute.

Coontz, S. (1992). *The way we never were: American families and the nostalgia trap.* New York: Basic Books.

Cooper, C. (1997). *Learner-centred assessment.* Launceston, Australia: Global Learning Communities.

Cowan, E. (1994). The enhancement of psychological wellness: Challenges and opportunities. *American Journal of Community Psychology, 22,* 149–179.

Cowan, E., Wyman, P., Work, W., & Iker, M. (1995). A preventive intervention for enhancing resilience among highly stressed urban children. *Journal of Primary Prevention, 15,* 247–283.

Crawford, D. & Bodine, R. (1996). *Conflict resolution education: A guide to implementing programs in schools, youth-serving organizations, and community and juvenile justice settings.* Washington, DC: U.S. Department of Justice and U.S. Department of Education.

Croninger, R. & Lee, V. (2001). Social capital and dropping out of high school: Benefits to at-risk students of teachers' support and guidance. *Teachers College Record, 103,* 548–581.

Csikszentmihalyi, M. (1990). *Flow: The psychology of optimal experience.* New York: HarperCollins.

Csikszentmihalyi, M. (1996). *Creativity: Flow and the psychology of discovery and invention.* New York: HarperCollins.

Csikszentmihalyi, M., Rathunde, K., Whalen, S., & Wong, M. (1994). *Talented teens: The roots of success and failure.* New York: HarperCollins

Curnan, S. & Hughes, D. (2002). Towards shared prosperity: Change-making in the CYD movement. *CYD Journal, 3* (1), 25–33.

Cutler, I. & Edwards, S. (2002). Linking youth and community development: Ideas from the Community Youth Development Initiative. *CYD Journal, 3*(1), 17–23.

Dalai Lama. (1998). *The art of happiness: A handbook for living.* New York: Penguin Putnam.

Dalianis, M. (1994). *Early trauma and adult resiliency: A midlife follow-up study of young children whose mothers were political prisoners during the Greek civil war.* Stockholm: Karolinska Institute.

Day, J. (1994). *Changing lives: Voices from a school that works.* Lanham: University Press of America, Inc.

Deci, E. (1995). *Why we do what we do: Understanding self-motivation.* New York: Penguin Books.

Deiro, J. (1996). *Teaching with heart: Making healthy connections with students.* Thousand Oaks, CA: Corwin Press.

Delpit, L. (1995). *Other people's children: Cultural conflict in the classroom.* New York: W.W. Norton.

Delpit, L. (1996). The politics of teaching literate discourse. In W. Ayers & P. Ford (Eds.), *City kids, city teachers: Reports from the front row.* New York: The New Press.

Diamond, M. & Hopson, J. (1998). *Magic trees of the mind: How to nurture your child's intelligence, creativity, and healthy emotions from birth through adolescence.* New York: Dutton.

Diehl, D. (2002). Family support America: Supporting "family supportive" evaluation. *The Evaluation Exchange, 8*(1), 14–15.

Donohue, M. & Benson, P. (1995). Religion and the well-being of adolescents. *Journal of Social Issues, 51,* 145–160.

Dossey, L. (2003). *Healing beyond the body: Medicine and the infinite reach of the mind.* Boston, MA: Shambala.

Dryfoos, J. (1998). *Safe passage: Making it through adolescence in a risky society.* New York: Oxford University Press.

Dryfoos, J. (2003). A community school in action. *Reclaiming Children and Youth: the Journal of Strength-Based Interventions, 11* (4), 203–205.

Durlak, J. (2000). Health promotion as a strategy in primary prevention. In D. Cicchetti, J. Rappaport, I. Sandler, & R. Weissberg (Eds.), *The promotion of wellness in children and adolescents* (pp. 221–241). Washington, DC: Child Welfare League Association Press.

Eccles, J. & Gootman, J. (2002). *Community programs to promote youth development.* Washington, DC: National Academies Press.

Eccles, J., Midgley, C., Buchanan, C., Wigfield, A., Reuman, D., & Maclver, D. (1993). Development during adolescence: The impact of stage-environment fit on young adolescents' experiences in schools and in families. *American Psychologist, 48*(2), 90–101.

Edelman, M. (1991, May-June). Kids first. *Mother Jones,* 31–32, 76–77.

Edmonds, R. (1986). Characteristics of effective schools. In U. Neisser (Ed.), *The school achievement of minority children: New perspectives.* Hillsdale, NJ: Lawrence Erlbaum.

Egeland, B., Carlson, E., & Sroufe, L. (1993). Resilience as process. *Development and Psychopathology, 5,* 517–528.

Eggert, L., Thompson, E., Herting, J., Nicholas, L., & Dicker, B. (1994). Preventing adolescent drug abuse and high school dropout through an intensive school-based social network development program. *American Journal of Health Promotion, 8*(3), 202–215.

Eisler, R. (2000). *Tomorrow's children: A blueprint for partnership education in the 21ˢᵗ century.* Boulder, CO: Westview.

Elias, M. & Weissberg, R. (2000). Wellness in schools: The grandfather tells a story. In D. Cicchetti, J. Rappaport, I. Sandler, & R. Weissberg (Eds.), *The promotion of wellness in children and adolescents* (pp. 243–269). Washington, DC: Child Welfare League Association Press.

Ellis, N. (2001, Summer). Tuning in. *Hope, 6,* 48–50, 61.

Emmons, R., Cheung, C., & Tehrani, K. (1998). Assessing spirituality through personal goals: Implications for research on religion and subjective well-being. *Social Indicators Research, 45,* 391–422.

Englander-Golden, P. (1991). *Say it straight: From compulsions to choices.* Palo Alto, CA: Science and Behavior Books.

Englander-Golden, P., Gitchel, E., Henderson, C., Golden, D., & Hardy, R. (2002). Say it straight training with mothers in chemical dependency treatment. *Journal of Offender Rehabilitation, 35,* 1–22.

Englander-Golden, P., Golden, D., Brookshire, W., Snow, C., Haag, M. & Chang, A. (1996). Communication skills program for prevention of risky behaviors. *Journal of Substance Misuse, I,* 38–46.

Epstein, K. (1998, March 4). An urban high school with no violence. *Education Week,* p. 45.

Erikson, E. (1963). *Childhood and society.* New York: W. W. Norton.

Erikson, E. (1968). *Identity: Youth and crisis.* London: Faber and Faber.

Eriksson, P.; Perfilieval, E.; Bjork-Eriksson, T.; Alborn, A.; Nordborg, C.; Peterson, D.A.; & Gage, F.H. (1998). Neurogenesis in the adult human hippocampus. *Nature Medicine, 4,* 1313-1317.

Esbensen, F., Deschenes, E., & Winfree, L., Jr. (1999). Differences between gang girls and gang boys: Results from a multisite survey. *Youth and Society, 31,* 27–53.

Esterling, B., L'Abate, L., Murray, E., & Pennebaker, J. (1999). Empirical foundations for writing in prevention and psychotherapy: Mental and physical health outcomes. *Clinical Psychology Review, 19,* 79–96.

Family Support America. (2000). *Family Support Centers, Volume I: Program planning and evaluation, A Program manager's toolkit.* Chicago: Family Support America.

Felner, R. (2000). Educational reform as ecologically-based prevention and promotion: The Project on High Performance Learning Communities. In D. Cicchetti, J. Rappaport, I. Sandler, & R. Weissberg (Eds.), *The promotion of wellness in children and adolescents* (pp. 271–307). Washington, DC: Child Welfare League Association Press.

Ferguson, Ronald. (1990). *The case for community-based programs that inform and motivate black male youth.* Washington, DC: The Urban Institute.

Festinger, T. (1984). *No one ever asked us: A postscript to the foster care system.* New York: Columbia University Press.

Finn, J., Gerber, S., Achilles, C., & Boyd-Zaharias, J. (2001). The enduring effects of small classes. *Teachers College Record, 103*(2), 145–183.

Frankl, V. (1984). *Man's search for meaning* (revised ed.). Boston: Pocket Books.

Freedman, M. (1993). *The kindness of strangers: Adult mentors, urban youth, and the new voluntarism.* San Francisco: Jossey-Bass.

Freire, P. (1993). *Education for critical consciousness.* New York: Continuum.

Fulbright-Anderson, K., Kubisch, A. & Connell, J. (Eds.). (1998). *New approaches to evaluating community initiatives: Volume 2, Theory, measurement, and analysis.* Washington, DC: Aspen Institute.

Fullan, M. (with S. Stiegelbauer). (1991). *The new meaning of educational change.* New York: Teachers College Press.

Fuller, B., Kagan, S., & Loeb, S. (2002). *New lives for poor families? Mothers and young children move through welfare reform.* Berkeley, CA; and Stanford, CA: Policy Analysis for California Education.

Furstenberg, F., Cook, T., Eccles, J., Elder, G., & Sameroff, A. (1998). *Managing to make it: Urban families and adolescent success.* Chicago: University of Chicago Press.

Gambone, M. (1998). Challenges of measurement in community change initiatives. In K. Fulbright-Anderson, A. Kubisch, & J. Connells (Eds.). *New approaches to evaluating community initiatives: Concepts, methods, and contexts,* (Volume 2, pp. 149–163). Washington, DC: Aspen Institute.

Gambone, M. & Arbreton, A. (1997). *Safe havens: The contributions of youth organizations to healthy adolescent development.* Philadelphia: Public/Private Ventures.

Gandara, P. (1995). *Over the ivy walls: The educational mobility of low income Chicanos.* New York: SUNY Press.

Garbarino, J., Dubrow, N., Kostelny, K. & Pardo, C. (1992). *Children in danger: Coping with the consequences of community violence.* San Francisco: Jossey-Bass.

Garcia, O. & Otheguy, R. (1995). The bilingual education of Cuban American children in Dade County's ethnic schools. In O. Garcia & C. Baker (Eds.), *Policy and practice in bilingual education: A reader extending the foundations* (pp. 93–102). Clevedon, UK: Multilingual Matters.

Gardner, H. (1993). *Multiple intelligences: The theory in practice.* New York: Basic Books.

Gardner, H. (1999). *The disciplined mind: What all students should understand.* New York: Simon and Schuster.

Gardner, H. (2000). *Intelligence reframed: Multiple intelligences for the 21ˢᵗ century.* New York: Basic Books.

Gardner, J. (1991, September). *Building community.* Paper prepared for the Leadership Studies Program. Washington, DC: Independent Sector.

Garmezy, N. (1974). The study of competence in children at risk for severe psychopathology. In E. Anthony (Ed.), *The child in his family, Volume 3: Children at psychiataric risk (*pp. 77–98). New York: John Wiley and Sons.

Garmezy, N. (1991). Resiliency and vulnerability to adverse developmental outcomes associated with poverty. *American Behavioral Scientist, 34,* 416–430.

Gibbs, J. (2001). *TRIBES: Discovering gifts in middle school.* Santa Rosa, CA: CenterSource.

Gibson, M. (1997). Complicating the immigrant/involuntary minority typology. *Anthropology & Education Quarterly, 28,* 431–454.

Gibson, M. (1997). Exploring and explaining the variability: Cross-national perspectives on the school performance of minority students. *Anthropology & Education Quarterly, 28,* 318–329.

Glasser, W. (1990). *The quality school: Managing students without coercion.* New York: Harper and Row.

Goldstein, J. (1994). *Insight meditation: The practice of freedom.* Boston, MA: Shambhala.

Goleman, D. (1995). *Emotional intelligence: Why it can matter more than I.Q.* New York: Bantam Books.

Gordon, E. & Song, L. (1994). Variations in the experience of resilience. In. M. Wang & E. Gorden (Eds.), *Educational resilience in inner-city America* (pp. 27–44). Hillsdale, NJ: Lawrence Erlbaum.

Gorman, D. (2002). The "science" of drug and alcohol prevention: The case of the randomized trial of the Life Skills Training program. *International Journal of Drug Policy, 13,* 21–26.

Greenberg, M., Domitrovich, C., & Bumbarger, B. (1999). *Preventing mental disorders in school-age children: A review of the effectiveness of prevention programs.* Rockville, MD: Center for Mental Health Services, U.S. Department of Health and Human Services.

Gregory, L. (1995). The "turnaround" process: Factors influencing the school success of urban youth. *Journal of Adolescent Research, 10,* 136–154.

Hakuta, K. & Beatty, A. (Eds.). (2000) *Testing English-language learners in U.S. schools: Reports and workshop summary.* Washington, DC: National Academies Press.

Halford, J. (1998–99). Longing for the sacred in schools: A conversation with Nel Noddings. *Educational Leadership, 56* (4), 28–32.

Halperin, S. (Ed.). (1988). *The forgotten half: Pathways to success for America's youth and young families.* Washington, DC: William T. Grant Foundation Commission on Work, Family, and Citizenship.

Halperin, S. (Ed.). (1998). *The forgotten half revisited: American youth and young families, 1988–2008* (pp. 1–26). Washington, DC: American Youth Policy Forum.

Hamovitch, B. (1996). Socialization without voice: An ideology of hope for at-risk students. *Teachers College Record, 98,* 286–306.

Harris, J. (1998). *The nurture assumption: Why children turn out the way they do.* New York: Touchstone.

Harter, S. (1990). Self and identity development. In S. Feldman & G. Elliott (Eds.), *At the threshold: The developing adolescent* (pp. 352–387). Cambridge, MA: Harvard University Press.

Hattie, J., Marsh, H., Neill, J., & Richards, G. (1997). Adventure education and Outward Bound: Out-of-class experiences that make a lasting difference. *Review of Educational Research, 67,* 43–87.

Heath, S. & McLaughlin, M. (Eds.). (1993). *Identity and inner-city youth: Beyond ethnicity and gender.* New York: Teachers College Press.

Heath, S., Soep, E., & Roach, A. (1998). Living the arts through language and learning: A report on community-based youth organizations. *Americans for the Arts Monographs, 2* (7).

Hemmings, A. (2000). Lona's links: Postoppositional identity work of urban youths. *Anthropology and Education Quarterly, 31,* 152–172.

Hendrick, S., & Hendrick, C. (2002). Love. In C. Snyder & S. Lopez (Eds.), *Handbook of positive psychology* (pp. 472–484). New York: Oxford University Press.

Henricson, C. & Roker, D. (2000). Support for the parents of adolescents: A review. *Journal of Adolescence, 23,* 763–783.

Henry, C., Sager, D., & Plunkett, S. (1996). Adolescents' perceptions of family system characteristics, parent-adolescent dyadic behaviors, adolescent qualities, and adolescent empathy. *Family Relations, 45,* 283–292.

Henry, T. (2002, May 22). Study: Arts education has academic effect. *USA Today On-Line.* Retrieved from http://www.usatoday.com

Heppner, P., & Lee, D. (2002). Problem-solving appraisal and psychological adjustment. In C. Snyder & S. Lopez (Eds.), *Handbook of positive psychology* (pp. 288–298). New York: Oxford University Press.

Herman, J. (1997). *Trauma and recovery.* New York: Basic Books.

Herman, M., Dornbusch, S., Herron, M. & Herting, J. (1997). The influence of family regulation, connection, and psychological autonomy on six measures of adolescent functioning. *Journal of Adolescent Research, 12,* 34–67.

Herrera, C., Sipe, C., & McClanahan, W. (2000). *Mentoring school-age children: Relationship development in community-based and school-based programs.* Philadelphia: Public/Private Ventures.

Hetherington, M. & Kelly, J. (2002). *For better or worse: Divorce reconsidered.* New York: Norton.

Heubert, J. & Hauser, R. (Eds.). (1999). *High stakes: Testing for tracking, promotion, and graduation.* Washington, DC: National Academies Press.

Higgins, G. (1994). *Resilient adults: Overcoming a cruel past.* San Francisco: Jossey-Bass.

Hill, K., Howell, J., Hawkins, J., & Battin-Pearson, S. (1999). Childhood risk factors for adolescent gang membership: Results from the Seattle Social Development Project. *Journal of Research in Crime and Delinquency, 36,* 300–322.

Hillman, J. (1996). *The soul's code: In search of character and calling.* New York: Random House.

hooks, b. (1994). *Teaching to transgress: Education as the practice of freedom.* New York: Routledge.

Howard, J. (1990). *Getting smart: The social construction of intelligence.* Lexington, MA: The Efficacy Institute.

Hyman, J. (1999). *Spheres of influence: A strategic synthesis and framework for community youth development.* Baltimore: Annie E. Casey Foundation.

Ianni, Francis. (1989). *The search for structure: A report on American youth today.* New York: Free Press.

Innovation Center for Community & Youth Development. (2002). Mission and goals. Madison, WI: University of Wisconsin.

Institute for Education in Transformation at the Claremont Graduate School. (1992). *Voices from the inside: A report on schooling from inside the classroom.* Bane, M. (Ed.) Claremont, CA: Author.

James, D. W., Jurich, S., & Estes, S. (2001). *Raising minority academic achievement: A compendium of education programs and practices.* Washington, DC: American Youth Policy Forum.

Jerald, C. (2001). Dispelling the myth revisited: Preliminary findings from a nationwide analysis of "high-flying" schools. Washington, DC: The Education Trust, Inc.

Johnson, D. & Johnson, R. (1989). *Cooperation and competition: Theory and research.* Edina, MN: Interaction Book Company.

Johnson, D. & Johnson, R. (1996). Conflict resolution and peer mediation programs in elementary and secondary schools: A review of the research. *Review of Educational Research, 66*(4), 459–506.

Kabat-Zinn, J. (1995). *Wherever you go, there you are: Mindfulness meditation in evreyday life.* New York: Hyperion.

Kagan, J. (1998). *Three seductive ideas.* Cambridge, MA: Harvard University Press.

Kaufman, J. & Zigler, E. (1987). Do abused children become abusive parents? *American Journal of Orthopsychiatry, 57,* 186–192.

Kessler, R. (2000). *The soul of education: Helping students find connection, compassion, and character at school.* Alexandria, VA: Association for Supervision and Curriculum Development.

Kilbourne, J. (1999). *Deadly persuasion: Why women and girls must fight the addictive power of advertising.* New York: Free Press.

Kim, U. & Chun, M. (1994). Educational "success" of Asian Americans: An indigenous perspective. *Applied Behavioral Development, 15,* 328–342.

Kitashima, M. (1997). Lessons from my life. *Resiliency in Action, 2*(3), 30–36.

Kohl, H. (1994). *"I won't learn from you" and other thoughts on creative maladjustment.* New York: The New Press.

Kohn, A. (1993). Choices for children: Why and how to let students decide. *Phi Delta Kappan, 74* (1), 9–20.

Kohn, A. (1996). *Beyond discipline: From compliance to community.* Alexandria, VA: Association for Supervision and Curriculum Development.

Kohn, A. (1997). The limits of teaching skills. *Reaching Today's Youth,* Summer, 14–16.

Kohn, A. (1999). *The schools our children deserve: Moving beyond traditional classrooms and "tougher standards."* Boston: Houghton Mifflin.

Kohn, A. (2000). *The case against standardized testing: Raising the scores, ruining the schools.* Portsmouth, NH: Heinemann.

Kreft, I. & Brown, J. (Eds.). (1998). The zero effects of drug prevention programs: Issues and solutions. *Evaluation Review. (Special Issue), 22.*

Kretzmann, J. & McKnight, J. (1993). *Building communities from the inside out.* Evanston, IL: Center for Urban Affairs and Policy Research, Northwestern University.

Kretzmann, J. & Schmitz, P. (1999). It takes a child to raise a whole village. *Resiliency in Action, 4*(2), 1, 3–4.

Kumpfer, K. (1999). Factors and processes contributing to resilience: The resilience framework. In M. Glantz & J. Johnson (Eds.), *Resilience and development: Positive life adaptations* (pp. 269–277). New York: Kluwer.

Kurcinka, M. (1992). *Raising your spirited child: A guide for parents whose child is more intense, sensitive, perceptive, persistent, and energetic.* New York: Perennial.

Laboratory Network Prgram. (2001). *Listening to student voices: Self-study toolkit.* Washington, DC: Office of Education and Research Improvement. Retrieved from http://www.nwrel.org/scpd/scc/studentvoices

Ladson-Billings, G. (1994). *Dreamkeepers: Successful teachers of African American children.* San Francisco: Jossey-Bass.

Lahey, B., Gordon, R., Loeber, R., Stouthamer-Loeber, M. & Farrington, D. (1999). Boys who join gangs: A prospective study of predictors of first gang entry. *Journal of Abnormal Child Psychology, 27,* 261–276.

Langer, E. (2002). Well-being: Mindfulness versus positive evaluation. In C. Snyder & S. Lopez (Eds.), *Handbook of positive psychology* (pp. 214–230). New York: Oxford University Press.

Larson, R. (2000). Toward a psychology of positive youth development. *American Psychologist, 55,* 170–183.

Layzer, J., Goodson, B., Bernstein, L., & Price, C. (2001). *National evaluation of family support programs: Final report.* Cambridge, MA: Abt Associates, Inc.

Lefcourt, H. (2001). *Humor: The psychology of living buoyantly.* New York: Plenum.

Lefcourt, H. (2002). Humor. In C. Snyder & S. Lopez (Eds.), *Handbook of positive psychology* (pp. 619–631). New York: Oxford University Press.

Levine, M. (2002). *Different minds learn differently.* New York: Simon and Schuster.

Lewis, T., Amini, F., & Lannon, R. (2000). *A general theory of love.* New York: Random House.

Locke, E. (2002). Setting goals for life and happiness. In C. Snyder & S. Lopez (Eds.), *Handbook of positive psychology* (pp. 299–312). New York: Oxford University Press.

Lofquist, W. (1992). Let's create a new culture of youth work in America. *New Designs for Youth Development,* Winter, 23–27.

Loutzenheiser, L. (2002). Being seen and heard: Listening to young women in alternative schools. *Anthropology & Education Quarterly, 33,* 441–464.

Lozoff, B. (2000). *It's a meaningful life—It just takes practice.* New York: Viking.

Luthar, S. & Burak, J. (2000). Adolescent wellness: In the eye of the beholder? In D. Cicchetti, J. Rappaport, I. Sandler, & R. Weissberg (Eds.), *The promotion of wellness in children and adolescents* (pp. 29–57). Washington, DC: Child Welfare League Association Press.

Luthar, S. & McMahon, T. (1996). Peer reputation among adolescents: Use of the Revised Class Play with inner-city teens. *Journal of Research on Adolescence, 6,* 581–603.

Luthar, S. & Zigler, E. (1992). Intelligence and social competence among high-risk adolescents. *Development and Psychopathology, 4,* 287–299.

MacBeath, J., Boyd, B., Rand, J., & Bell, S. (1995). *Schools speak for themselves: Toward a framework for self-evaluation* (pp. 28–29). London: The National Union of Teachers.

Maddux, J. (2002). Self-efficacy: The power of believing you can. In C. Snyder & S. Lopez (Eds.), *Handbook of positive psychology* (pp. 277–287). New York: Oxford University Press.

Males, M. (1996). *The scapegoat generation: American's war on adolescence.* Monroe, ME: Common Courage Press.

Males, M. (1999). *Framing youth: 10 myths about the next generation.* Monroe, ME: Common Courage Press.

Marshall, K. (1998). Reculturing systems with resilience/health realization. *Promoting Positive and Healthy Behaviors in Children: Fourteenth Annual Rosalynn Carter Symposium on Mental Health Policy* (pp. 48–58). Atlanta, GA: The Carter Center.

Maslow, A. (1954). *Motivation and personality.* New York: Harper and Row.

Masten, A. (1994). Resilience in individual development: Successful adaptation despite risk and adversity. In M. Wang & E. Gorden (Eds.), *Educational resilience in inner-city America* (pp. 3–25). Hillsdale, NJ: Lawrence Erlbaum.

Masten, A. (2001). Ordinary magic: Resilience processes in development. *American Psychologist, 56,* 227–238.

Masten, A. & Coatsworth, D. (1998). The development of competence in favorable and unfavorable environments: Lessons from research on successful children. *American Psychologist, 53,* 205–220.

Masten, A., Hubbard, J., Gest, S., Tellegen, A., Garmezy, N., & Ramirez, M. (1999). Competence in the context of adversity: Pathways to resilience and maladaptation from childhood to late adolescence. *Development and Psychopathology, 11,* 143–169.

Masten, A. & Reed, M. (2002). Resilience in development. In C. Snyder & S. Lopez (Eds.), *Handbook of positive psychology* (pp. 74–88). New York: Oxford University Press.

Maton, K. & Wells, E. (1995). Religion as a community resource for well-being: Prevention, healing, and empowerment pathways. *Journal of Social Issues, 51,* 177–193.

McBroom, P. (2002, September 20). Positive emotions, including laughter are important paths out of trauma, according to UC Berkeley psychologist. *Campus News.*

McCullough, M. & Witvliet, C. (2002). The psychology of forgiveness. In C. Snyder & S. Lopez (Eds.), *Handbook of positive psychology* (pp. 446–458). New York: Oxford University Press.

McDonald, L. & Moberg, P. (2000). Families and Schools Together: FAST strategies for increasing involvement of all parents in schools and preventing drug abuse. In W. Hansen, S. Giles, & M. Fearnow-Kenney (Eds.), *Improving prevention effectiveness* (pp. 235–250). Greensboro, NC: Tanglewood Research.

McFarlane, A., Bellissimo, A., & Norman, G. (1995). Family structure, family functioning and adolescent well-being: The transcendent influence of parental style. *Journal of Child Psychology and Psychiatry, 36,* 847–865.

McKnight, J. (1992, Winter). Mapping community capacity. *New Designs for Youth Development,* 9–15.

McLaughlin, M. (2000). *Community counts.* New York: Public Education Network.

McLaughlin, M., Irby, M., & Langman, J. (1994). *Urban sanctuaries: Neighborhood organizations in the lives and futures of inner-city youth.* San Francisco: Jossey-Bass.

McLaughlin, M. & Talbert, J. (1993). *Contexts that matter for teaching and learning.* Stanford, CA: Stanford University.

McLaughlin, M. & Talbert, J. (2001). *Professional communities and the work of high school teaching.* Chicago: University of Chicago Press.

McNeely, C., Nonnemaker, J., & Blum, R. (2002). Promoting school connectedness: Evidence from the National Longitudinal Study of Adolescent Health. *Journal of School Health, 72*(4), 138–146.

Mehan, H., Hubbard, L., & Villanueva. (1994). Forming academic identities: Accommodation without assimilation. *Anthropology and Education Quarterly, 25,* 91–117.

Meier, D. (1995). *The power of their ideas.* Boston: Beacon Press.

Meier, D. (2000). *Will standards save public education?* Boston: Beacon Press.

Meier, D. (2002). *In schools we trust: Creating communities of learning in an era of testing and standardization.* Boston: Beacon Press.

Melchior, A. (1996). *National evaluation of Learn and Serve America school and community-based programs: Interim report: Appendices.* Washington, DC: Corporation for National and Community Service.

Melchior, A. (1998). *National evaluation of Learn and Serve America school and community-based programs: Final report.* Washington, DC: Corporation for National and Community Service.

Miller, A. (1990). *The untouched key: Tracing childhood trauma in creativity.* New York: Anchor Books.

Miller, R. (1995), *What are schools for? Holistic education in American culture.* Brandon, VT: Holistic Education Press.

Mills, R. (1993). *The health realization model: A community empowerment primer.* Alhambra, CA: California School of Professional Psychology.

Mills, R. (1995). *Realizing mental health: Toward a new psychology of resiliency.* New York: Sulzburger and Graham Publishing.

Mills, R. & Spittle, E. (2001). *Wisdom within.* Auburn, WA: Lone Pine Publishing.

Moore, J. (1991). *Going down to the barrio: Homeboys and homegirls in change.* Philadelphia: Temple University Press.

Moorman, C. (2001). *Spirit whisperers: Teachers who nourish a child's spirit.* Merrill, MI: Personal Power Press.

Morrison, G., Robertson, L., Laurie, B., & Kelly, J. (2002). Protective factors related to antisocial behavior trajectories. *Journal of Clinical Psychology, 58,* 277–290.

Morrison Institute for Public Policy. (1995). *Schools, communities, and the arts: A research compendium.* Tempe, AZ: Arizona State University.

Morrow, K. & Styles, M. (1995, May). *Building relationships with youth in program settings: A study of Big Brothers Big Sisters.* Philadelphia: Public/Private Ventures.

Muller, W. (1996). *How, then, shall we live? Four simple questions that reveal the beauty and meaning of our lives.* New York: Bantam Books.

Multon, K., Brown, S., & Lent, R. (1991). Relation of self-efficacy beliefs to academic outcomes: A meta-analytic investigation. *Journal of Counseling Psychology, 18,* 30–31.

Nakamura, J., & Csikszentmihalyi, M. (2002). The concept of flow. In C. Snyder & S. Lopez (Eds.), *Handbook of positive psychology* (pp. 89–105). New York: Oxford University Press.

Nathan, J. (1991). An interview with Herb Kohl: Toward educational change and economic justice. *Phi Delta Kappan, 72,* 678–681.

National Association of Elementary School Principals. (2001). Survey of After-school Programs. Washington, DC: NAESP.

National Commission on Service-Learning. (2002). *Learning in deed: The power of service-learning for American schools.* Battle Creek, MI: W.K. Kellogg Foundation.

National 4-H Council. (2002). *The national conversation on youth development in the 21ˢᵗ century: Final report.* Chevy Chase, MD: National 4-H Council.

Newcomb, M. & Bentler, P. (1988). *Consequences of adolescent drug use: Impact on the lives of young adults.* New York: Books on Demand.

Nieto, S. (1992). *Affirming diversity: The sociopolitical context of multicultural education.* New York: Longman.

Nieto, S. (1994). Lessons from students on creating a chance to dream. *Harvard Educational Review, 64,* 392–426.

Noddings, N. (1988, December 7). Schools face crisis in caring. *Education Week,* p. 32.

Noddings, N. (1992). *The challenge to care in schools: An alternative approach to education.* New York: Teachers College Press.

Oakes, J. (1985). *Keeping track: How schools structure inequality.* New Haven: Yale University Press.

Oetting, E. (1993). Orthogonal cultural identification: Theoretical links between cultural identification and substance use. In M. Delarosa & J. Reicio Adrados (Eds.), *Drug abuse among minority youth: Methodological issues and recent research advances* (pp. 32–56). Bethesda, MD: National Institute on Drug Abuse.

O'Gorman, P. (1994). *Dancing backwards in high heels: How women master the art of resilience.* Center City, MN: Hazeldon.

Ohanian, S. (1999). *One size fits few: The folly of educational standards.* Portsmouth, NH: Heinemann.

O'Leary, V. & Ickovics, J. (1995). Resilience and thriving in response to challenge: An opportunity for a paradigm shift in women's health. *Women's Health: Research on Gender, Behavior, and Policy, 1,* 121–142.

Oliner, S. & Oliner, P. (1989). *The roots of altruism.* New York: American Jewish Committee.

Olsen, L. (1998). *Made in America: Immigrant students in our public schools.* New York: The New Press.

Ornstein, R. & Sobel, D. (1999). *The healing brain: Breakthrough discoveries about how the brain keeps us healthy.* Cambridge, MA: Malor Books.

Owens, J. (2002, February 20). Breaking new ground: Two neighborhood studies on crime, children aim to change policy, improve lives. *Chicago Tribune.* Retrieved from: http://phdcn.harvard.edu./news/tribune.html

Palmer, P. (1998). *The courage to teach: Exploring the inner landscape of a teacher's life.* San Francisco, CA: Jossey-Bass.

Panel on High-Risk Youth, National Research Council. (1993). *Losing generations: Adolescents in high-risk settings.* Washington, DC: National Academies Press.

Pargament, K. (1997). *The psychology of religion and coping: Theory, research, practice.* New York: Guilford.

Pargament, K., & Mahoney, A. (2002). Spirituality: Discovering and conserving the sacred. In C. Snyder & S. Lopez (Eds.), *Handbook of positive psychology* (pp. 646–659). New York: Oxford University Press.

Pariser, E. (2001). Relational education: An open letter to an educator. *Paths of learning: Options for families & communities, 8,* 35–42.

Patterson, J. (2002). Understanding family resilience. *Journal of Clinical Psychology, 58,* 233–246.

Pearce, J. (1977/1992). *Magical child.* New York: Plume Books.

Peng, S. (1994). Understanding resilient students: The use of national longitudinal databases. In. M. Wang & E. Gorden (Eds.), *Educational resilience in inner-city America* (pp. 73–84). Hillsdale, NJ: Lawrence Erlbaum.

Pennebaker, J., Colder, M., & Sharp, L. (1990). Accelerating the coping process. *Journal of Personality and Social Psychology, 58,* 528–537.

Perry, C. (1989). Prevention of alcohol use and abuse in adolescence: Teacher vs. peer-led intervention. *Crisis, 10*(10), 52–61.

Pert, C. (1997). *Molecules of emotion: The science behind mind-body medicine.* New York: Touchstone.

Peterson, C. (2000). The future of optimism. *American Psychologist, 55,* 44–55.

Peterson, C. & Seligman, M. (2003). Values in action (VIA) classification of strengths. Washington, DC: American Psychological Association; Oxford, UK: Oxford University Press. Draft retrieved April 11, 2003, from http://www.positivepsychology.org/taxonomy.htm

Peterson, C., & Steen, T. (2002). Optimistic explanatory style. In C. Snyder & S. Lopez (Eds.), *Handbook of positive psychology* (pp. 244–256). New York: Oxford University Press.

Peterson, K. (2002, January 13). Divorce need not end in disaster. *USA Today.*

Phelan, P., Davidson, A., & Cao, H. (1992). Speaking up: Students' perspectives on school. *Phi Delta Kappan, 73* 695–704.

Phinney, J. & Rosenthal, D. (1992). Ethnic identity in adolescence: Process, context, and outcome. In G. Adams, T. Bullotta, & R. Montemayor (Eds.), *Adolescent identity formation (*pp. 145–172). Newbury Park, CA: Sage.

Pianta, R. (1999). *Enhancing relationships between children and teachers.* Washington, DC: American Psychological Association.

Pittman, K. & Irby, M. (1998). Reflections on a decade of promoting youth development. In S. Halperin (Ed.), *The forgotten half revisited: American youth and young families, 1988–2008* (pp. 159–170). Washington, DC: American Youth Policy Forum.

Pittman, K. & Zeldin, S. (1995). *Premises, principles, and practices: Defining the why, what, and how of promoting youth development through organizational practice.* Washington, DC: Academy for Educational Development, Center for Youth Development & Policy Research.

Polakow, V. (1993). *Lives on the edge: Single mothers and their children in the other America.* Chicago: University of Chicago Press.

Popham, W. J. (2001). *The truth about testing: An educator's call to action.* Alexandria, VA: Association for Supervision and Curriculum Development.

Poplin, M. & Weeres, J. (1992). *Voices from the inside: A report on schooling from inside the classroom.* Claremont, CA: School of Educational Studies, Claremont Graduate University.

Portner, J. (1994, April 6). The search for elusive sanctuaries for urban youth. *Education Week,* 30–31.

Pransky, G. (1998). *Renaissance of psychology.* New York: Sulzburger & Graham Publishing.

President's Advisory Commission on Educational Excellence for Hispanic Americans. (2000). *Testing Hispanic students in the United States: Technical and policy issues.* Washington, DC: President's Advisory Commission on Educational Excellence for Hispanic Americans.

Pringle, B., Anderson, L., Rubenstein, M., & Russo, A. (1993). *Peer tutoring and mentoring services for disadvantaged secondary school students: An evaluation of the secondary schools basic skills demonstration assistance program.* Washington, DC: Policy Studies Associates.

Public Agenda. (1997). *Kids these days: What Americans really think about the next generation.* New York: Public Agenda.

Purkey, W. (1995). *Inviting school success: A self-concept approach to teaching, learning, and democratic practice.* Florence, KY: Wadsworth.

Putnam, R. (2000). *Bowling alone: The collapse and revival of American community.* New York: Simon and Schuster.

Quinton, D, Pickeles, A., Maughan, B., & Rutter, M. (1993). Partners, peers, and pathway: Assortive pairing and continuities in conduct disorder. *Development and Psychopathology, 5,* 763–783.

Rak, C. (2002). Heroes in the nursery: Three case studies in resilience. *Journal of Clinical Psychology, 58,* 247–260.

Rein, G., McCraty, R., & Atkinson, M. (1995). The physiological and psychological effects of compassion and anger. *Journal of Advancement in Medicine, 8,* 87–105.

Resnick, M., Bearman, P., Blum, R., Bauman, K., Harris, K., Jones, J., Tabor, J., Beuring, T., Sieving, R., Shew, M., Ireland, M., Bearinger, L., & Udry, J. (1997). Protecting adolescents from harm: Findings from the National Longitudinal Study on Adolescent Health. *Journal of the American Medical Association, 278,* 823–832.

Rich, D. (1998). *MegaSkills: Building children's achievement for the information age.* New York: Houghton-Mifflin.

Richardson, G. (2002). The metatheory of resilience and resiliency. *Journal of Clinical Psychology, 58,* 307–321.

Richters, J. & Martinez, P. (1993). Violent communities, family choices, and children's chances: An algorithm for improving the odds. *Development and Psychopathology, 5,* 609–627.

Rhodes, W. & Brown, W. (Eds.). (1991). *Why some children succeed despite the odds.* New York: Praeger.

Roaf, P., Tierney, J., & Hunte, D. (1994, Fall). *Big Brothers/Big Sisters: A study of volunteer recruitment and screening.* Philadelphia: Public/Private Ventures.

Roberts, W. & Strayer, J. (1996). Empathy, emotional expressiveness, and prosocial behavior. *Child Development, 67,* 449–470.

Rockwell, S. (1998). Overcoming four myths that prevent fostering resilience. *Reaching Today's Youth: The Community Circle of Caring Journal, 2*(3), 14–17.

Rogoff, B. (2003). *The cultural nature of human development.* New York: Oxford University Press.

Oxford University Press. Ross, E. (2003, January 26). One parent, twice the trouble. *Contra Costa Times.*

RPP International. (1998). *An evaluation of K–12 service-learning in California.* Sacramento: California Department of Education.

Rubin, L. (1996). *The transcendent child: Tales of triumph over the past.* New York: Basic Books.

Rutter, M. (1979). Protective factors in children's responses to stress and disadvantage. In M. Kent & J. Rolf (Eds.), *Primary prevention of psychopathology, Vol. 3: Social competence in children* (pp. 49–74). Hanover, NH: University Press of New England.

Rutter, M. (1987). Psychosocial resilience and protective mechanisms. *American Journal of Orthopsychiatry, 57,* 316–331.

Rutter, M. (1989). Pathways from childhood to adult life. *Journal of Child Psychology and Psychiatry, 30,* 23–54.

Rutter, M. (2000). Resilience reconsidered: Conceptual considerations, empirical findings and policy implications. In J.P. Shonkoff and S.J. Meisels (eds.), *Handbook of Early Childhood Intervention, 2nd ed.,* 651-682. New York: Cambridge University Press.

Rutter, M., Maughan, B., Mortimore, P., Ouston, J., & Smith, A. (1979). *Fifteen thousand hours: Secondary schools and their effects on children.* Cambridge, MA: Harvard University Press.

Rutter, M. & Quinton, D. (1984). Long-term follow-up of women institutionalized in childhood: Factors promoting good functioning in adult life. *British Journal of Developmental Psychology, 2,* 191–204.

Ryan, A. (2001). The peer group as a context for the development of young adolescent motivation and achievement. *Child Development, 72,* 1135–1150.

Ryan, R. & Deci, E. (2000). Self-determination theory and the facilitation of intrinsic motivation, social development, and well-being. *American Psychologist, 55,* 68–78.

Ryff, C., Singer, B., Love, G., & Essex, M. (1998). Resilience in adulthood and later life: Defining features and dynamic processes. In J. Lomranz (Ed.), *Handbook of aging and mental health: An integrative approach* (pp. 69–96). New York: Plenum.

Sacks, P. (1999). *Standardized minds: The high price of America's testing culture and what we can do to change it.* Cambridge: Perseus Books.

Safer, M. (On-air Reporter). (1995). Too good to be true. *60 Minutes* [Television broadcast]. New York: Columbia Broadcasting System.

Sale, E. & Springer, F. (2001). Prevention works! The recent national cross-site evaluation of high-risk youth programs reveals the "how" and "why" of prevention. *Prevention Tactics 4*(3), 1–8.

Saleebey, D. (Ed.). (2001). *The strengths perspective in social work practice* (3rd ed.). Boston: Allyn Bacon.

Salzberg, S. (2002). *Faith: Trusting your own deepest experience.* New York: Riverhead Books.

Sampson, R., Raudenbush, S., & Earls, F. (1997). Neighborhoods and violent crime: A multilevel study of collective efficacy. *Science, 277,* 918–924.

Sanders, M. (1997). Overcoming obstacles: Academic achievement as a response to racism and discrimination. *Journal of Negro Education, 66,* 83–93.

Sandler, I. (2001). Quality and ecology of adversity as common mechanisms of risk and resilience. *American Journal of Community Psychology, 29,* 19–61.

Sarason, S. (1990). *The predictable failure of educational reform.* San Francisco: Jossey-Bass.

Scales, P. & Leffert, N. (1999). *Developmental assets: A synthesis of the scientific research on adolescent development.* Minneapolis, MN: Search Institute.

Schon, D. (1990). *Educating the reflective practitioner: Toward a new design for teaching and learning in the profession.* San Francisco: Jossey-Bass.

Schor, I. (1993). Education is politics: Paulo Freire's critical pedagogy. In P. McLaren & P. Leonard (Eds.), *Paulo Freire: A Critical Encounter* (pp. 25–35). London: Routledge.

Schorr, L. (1988). *Within our reach: Breaking the cycle of disadvantage.* New York: Anchor Books.

Schorr, L. (1997). *Common purpose: Strengthening families and neighborhoods to rebuild America.* New York: Anchor Books.

Schulman, M. (2002). The passion to know: A developmental perspective. In C. Snyder & S. Lopez (Eds.), *Handbook of positive psychology* (pp. 313–326). New York: Oxford University Press.

Schunk, D. (1989). Self-efficacy and achievement behaviors. *Educational Psychologist, 1,* 173–208.

Schunk, D. (1991). Self-efficacy and achievement motivation. *Educational Psychologist, 26,* 207–231.

Scribner, A. & Scribner, J. (2001, December). High-performing schools serving Mexican American students: What they can teach us. *ERIC Digest* ED459048. Retrieved from http://www.ed.gov/databases/ERIC_Digests/ed459048.html.

Schwarzer, R. & Fuchs, R. (1995). Changing risk behaviors and adopting health behaviors: The role of self-efficacy beliefs. In A. Bandura (Ed.), *Self-efficacy in changing societies* (pp. 259–288). Cambridge, UK: Cambridge University Press.

Schweinhart, L., Barnes, H., & Wiekart, D. (1993). *Significant benefits: The High/Scope Perry Preschool study through age 27.* Ypsilanti, MI: High/Scope Press.

Schweinhart, L. & Weikart, D. (1997a). Child-initiated learning in preschool: Prevention that works! *High/Scope Resource, 16*(2), 1, 9–11.

Schweinhart, L. & Weikart, D. (1997b). The High/Scope preschool curriculum comparison study through age 23. *Early Childhood Research Quarterly, 12,* 117–143.

Schweinhart, L. & Weikart, D. (1997c). *Lasting differences: The High/Scope preschool curriculum comparison study through age 23.* Ypsilanti, MI: High/Scope Press.

Secretary's Commission on Achieving Necessary Skills. (SCANS) Report, U.S. Department of Labor. (2000). *Learning a living: A blueprint for high performance.* Baltimore: The Johns Hopkins University Institute for Policy Studies. Retrieved from http://wdr.doleta.gov/SCANS/lal/LAL.HTM

Seita, J., Mitchell, M., & Tobin, C. (1996). *In whose best interest: One child's odyssey, a nation's responsibility.* Elizabethtown, PA: Continental Press.

Seligman, M. (1992/1998). *Learned optimism: How to change your mind and your life.* New York: Pocket Books.

Seligman, M. (2002). Positive psychology, positive prevention, and positive therapy. In C. Snyder & S. Lopez (Eds.), *Handbook of positive psychology* (pp. 3–9). New York: Oxford University Press.

Seligman, M., Reivich, K., Jaycox, L., & Gillham, J. (1995). *The optimistic child: A revolutionary program that safeguards children against depression and builds lifelong resilience.* Boston: Houghton Mifflin.

Senge, P., Cambron-McCabe, N., Lucas, T., Smith, B., Dutton, J., & Kleiner, A. (Eds.). (2000). *Schools that learn.* New York: Doubleday.

Sergiovanni, T. (1996). *Leadership for the schoolhouse.* San Francisco: Jossey-Bass.

Sergiovanni, T. (2000). *The lifeworld of leadership: Creating culture, community, and personal meaning in our schools.* San Francisco: Jossey-Bass.

Shannon, P. (1995). *Text, lies, and videotape.* Portsmouth, NH: Heinemann.

Shapiro, S., Schwartz, G. & Santerre, C. (2002). Meditation and positive psychology. In C. Snyder & S. Lopez (Eds.), *Handbook of positive psychology* (pp. 632–645). New York: Oxford University Press.

Simonton, D. (2000). Creativity: Cognitive, personal development, and social aspects. *American Psychologist, 55,* 151–158.

Simonton, D. (2002). Creativity. In C. Snyder & S. Lopez (Eds.), *Handbook of positive psychology* (pp. 189–201). New York: Oxford University Press.

Sipe, C., & Roder, A. (1999). *Mentoring school-age children: A classification of programs.* Philadelphia: Public/Private Ventures.

Slavin, R. (1990). *Cooperative learning: Theory, research, and practice.* Englewood Cliffs, NJ: Prentice Hall.

Slavin, R. (1995). Enhancing intergroup relations in schools: Cooperative learning and other strategies. In W. Hawley & A. Jackson (Eds.), *Toward a common destiny: Improving Race and ethnic relations in America* (pp. 291–314). San Francisco, CA: Jossey-Bass.

Sleeter, C. & McLaren, P. (Eds.). (1995). *Multicultural education, cultural pedagogy, and the politics of difference.* Albany, NY: SUNY Press.

Snyder, C. (Ed.). (2000). *Handbook of hope: Theory, measures, and applications.* San Diego: Academic Press.

Snyder, C. & Lopez, S. (Eds.). (2002). *Handbook of positive psychology.* New York: Oxford University Press.

Snyder, C., Rand, K., & Sigmon, D. (2002). Hope theory: A member of the positive psychology family. In C. Snyder & S. Lopez (Eds.), *Handbook of positive psychology* (pp. 257–276). New York: Oxford University Press.

Steinberg, L. (2000). The family at adolescence: Transition and transformation. *Journal of Adolescent Health, 27,* 170–178.

Steinberg, L., Brown, B., & Dornbusch, S. (1997). *Beyond the classroom: Why school reform has failed and what parents need to do.* New York: Touchstone.

Stevenson, R. & Ellsworth, J. (1993). Drop-outs and the silencing of critical voices. In L. Weis & M. Fine (Eds.), *Beyond silenced voices: Class, race, and gender in United States schools* (pp. 259–272). New York: SUNY Press.

Stohlberg, A. & Mahler, J. (1994). Enhancing treatment gains in a school-based intervention for children of divorce through skill training, parental involvement, and transfer procedures. *Journal of Consulting and Clinical Psychology, 62,* 147–156.

Strayhorn, J. (1988). *The competent child: An approach to psychotherapy and preventive mental health.* New York: Guilford.

Study Circles Resource Center. (2001). *Organizing community-wide dialogue for action and change.* Pomfret, CT: Topsfield Foundation.

Swadener, B. & Lubeck, S. (1995). *Children and families "at promise": Deconstructing the discourse of risk.* Albany, NY: SUNY Press.

Sylwester, R. (1998). Art for the brain's sake. *Educational Leadership, 56*(3), 31–35.

Talbert, J. & Wallin, M. (2001). *Professional communities and the work of high school teaching.* Chicago: University of Chicago Press.

Taylor, S., Kemeny, M., Reed, G., Bower, J., & Gruenewald, T. (2000). Psychological resources, positive illusions, and health. *American Psychologist, 55,* 99–109.

TCWF Newsletter. (1999). Youth lead the way to healthier communities. Retrieved from http://www.tcwf.org/newslttr/summer99/pages/page1.htm

Thompson, S. (2002). The role of personal control in adaptive functioning. In C. Snyder & S. Lopez (Eds.), *Handbook of positive psychology* (pp. 202–213). New York: Oxford University Press.

Thornberry, T. (1998). Membership in youth gangs and involvement in serious and violent offending. In R. Loeber & D. Farrington (Eds.), *Serious and violent offenders: Risk factors and successful interventions* (pp. 147–166). Thousand Oaks: Sage.

Tierney, J., Grossman, J., & Resch, N. (1995). *Making a difference: An impact study of Big Brothers/Big Sisters.* Philadelphia: Public/Private Ventures.

Tindall, J. (1995). *Peer programs: An in-depth look at peer helping.* Bristol, PA: Accelerated Development.

Tobler, N., Roona, M., Ochshorn, P., Marshall, D., Streke, A., & Stackpole, K. (2000). School-based adolescent drug prevention programs: 1998 meta-analysis. *Journal of Primary Prevention, 20,* 275–336.

Trumbull, E., Rothstein-Fisch, C., Greenfield, P., & Quiroz, B. (2001). *Bridging cultures between home and school: A guide for teachers.* Mahwah, NJ: Lawrence Erlbaum Associates, Inc.

Turner, R.J., Lloyd, D., & Roszcll, P. (1999). Personal resources and the social distribution of depression. *American Journal of Community Psychology, 27,* 643–672.

U.S. Department of Education and U.S. Department of Justice. (1998). *Safe and smart: Making the after-school hours work for kids.* Washington, DC: Retrieved from http://ed.gov/pubs/SafeandSmart

Vaillant, G. (2000). Adaptive mental mechanisms: Their role in a positive psychology. *American Psychologist, 55,* 89–98.

Vaillant, G. (2002). *Aging well: Surprising guideposts to a happier life from the landmark harvard study of adult development.* Boston: Little, Brown, and Company.

Valenzuela, A. (1999). *Subtractive schooling: U.S.-Mexican youth and the politics of caring.* Albany, NY: SUNY Press.

Vande Berg, D. & Van Bockern, S. (1995). Building resilience through humor. *Reclaiming Children and Youth, 4*(3), 26–29.

Vasquez, G. (2000). Resiliency: Juvenile offenders recognize their strengths to change their lives. *Corrections Today, 62*(3), 106–110, 125.

Vigil, J. D. (1990). Cholos and gangs: Culture change and street youth in Los Angeles. In R. Huff (Ed.), *Gangs in America: Diffusion, diversity, and public policy* (pp. 146–162). Thousand Oaks, CA: Sage.

Wagner, M. & Golan, S. (1996). *California's Healthy Start school-linked services initiative: Summary of evaluation findings.* Menlo Park, CA: SRI International.

Walker, K. & Arbreton, A. (2002). *Working together to build beacon centers in San Francisco: Evaluation findings from 1998–2000.* Phildelphia, PA: Public/Private Ventures.

Walker-Barnes, C. & Mason, C. (2001). Ethnic differences in the effect of parenting on gang involvement and gang delinquency: A longitudinal, hierarchical linear modeling perspective. *Child Development, 72,* 1814–1831.

Wallerstein, J., Blakeslee, S., & Lewis, J. (2000). *The unexpected legacy of divorce: A 25 year landmark study.* New York: Hyperion.

Wallerstein, N. (1992). Powerlessness, empowerment, and health: Implications for health promotion programs. *American Journal of Health Promotion, 6,* 197–205.

Walsh, F. (1998). *Strengthening family resilience.* New York: Guilford.

Walsh, J. (1997). *Stories of renewal: Community building and the future of urban America.* New York: Rockefeller Foundation.

Wasley, P., Fine, M., Gladden, M., Holland, N., King, S., Mosak, E., & Powell, L. (2000). *Small schools, great strides: A study of new small schools in Chicago.* New York: Bank Street College of Education.

Wasley, P., Hampel, R., & Clark, R. (1997). *Kids and school reform.* San Francisco: Jossey-Bass.

Waterman, A. (1992). Identity as an aspect of optimal psychological functioning. In G. Adams, T. Bullotta, & R. Montemayor (Eds.), *Adolescent identity formation* (pp. 50–72). Newbury Park, CA: Sage.

Watson, M. & Ecken, L. (2003). *Learning to trust: Transforming difficult elementary classrooms through developmental discipline.* San Francisco: Jossey-Bass.

Watt, N., Anthony, E., Wynne, L. & Rolf, J. (Eds.) (1984). *Children at risk for schizophrenia: A longitudinal perspective.* New York: Cambridge University Press.

Watt, N., David, J., Ladd, K., & Shamos, S. (1995). The life course of psychological resilience: A phenomenological perspective on deflecting life's slings and arrows. *Journal of Primary Prevention, 15,* 209–246.

Weinstein, R. (2002). *Reaching higher: The power of expectations in schooling.* Cambridge, MA: Harvard University Press.

Weinstein, R. & McGown, C. (1998). Expectancy effects in "context": Listening to the voices of students and teachers. In J. Brophy (Ed.), *Advances in research on teaching: Expectations in the classroom,* (Volume 7, pp. 215–242). Greenwich, CT: JAI Press.

Weinstein, R., Soule, C., Collins, F., Cone, J., Mehlhorn, M., & Simontacchi, K. (1991). Expectations and high school change: Teacher-researcher collaboration to prevent school failure. *American Journal of Community Psychology, 19,* 333–363.

Weitoft, G., Hjern, A., Haglund, B., & Rosen, M. (2003). Mortality, severe morbidity, and injury in children living with single parents in Sweden: A population-based study. *Lancet, 361* (9354). Retrieved from http://www.thelancet.com/journal/vol361/iss9354

Weitz, J. (1996). *Coming up taller: Arts and humanities programs for children and youth at risk.* Washington, DC: President's Committee on the Arts and the Humanities.

Wenglinsky, H. (2000). *How teaching matters.* Princeton, NJ: Educational Testing Service.

Werner, E. (1986). Resilient offspring of alcoholics: A longitudinal study from birth to age 18. *Journal of Studies on Alcohol, 14,* 34–40.

Werner, E. (1995). *Pioneer children on the journey west.* Boulder, CO: Westview Press.

Werner, E. (1996). How kids become resilient: Observations and cautions. *Resiliency in Action 1,* 1: 18–28.

Werner, E. (1998). *Reluctant witnesses: Children's voices from the Civil War.* Boulder, CO: Westview Press.

Werner, E. (2000a). Protective factors and individual resilience. In J. Shonkoff & S. Meisels (Eds.), *Handbook of early childhood intervention* (pp. 115–132). New York: Cambridge University Press.

Werner, E. (2000b). *Through the eyes of innocents: Children witness World War II.* Boulder, CO: Westview Press.

Werner, E. & Smith, R. (1982). *Vulnerable but invincible: A longitudinal study of resilient children and youth.* New York: McGraw Hill.

Werner, E. & Smith, R. (1992). *Overcoming the odds: High risk children from birth to adulthood.* New York: Cornell University Press.

Werner, E. & Smith, R. (2001). *Journeys from childhood to the midlife: Risk, resilience, and recovery.* New York: Cornell University Press.

WestEd (2002). *Resilience and Youth Development Module report.* San Francisco: Author.

Wheelock, A. (1992). *Crossing the tracks: How "untracking" can save America's schools.* New York: The New Press.

White, J. & Wehlage, G. (1995). Community collaboration: If it is such a good idea, why is it so hard to do? *Educational Evaluation and Policy Analysis, 17,* 23–28.

Wigfield, A. & Eccles, J. (Eds.) (2002). *Development of achievement motivation.* San Diego: Academic Press.

Wilkes, G. (2002). Abused child to nonabusive parent: Resilience and conceptual change. *Journal of Clinical Psychology, 58,* 261–278.

Williams, B. (Ed.). (1996/2003). *Closing the achievement gap: A vision for changing beliefs and practices.* Alexandria, VA: Association for Supervision and Curriculum Development.

Wilson, B. & Corbett, H. (2001). *Listening to urban kids: School reform and the teachers they want.* New York: SUNY Press.

Wolin, S. & Wolin, S. (1993). *The resilient self: How survivors of troubled families rise above adversity.* New York: Villard Books.

Wyman, P., Cowen, E., Work, W., Hoyt-Meyers, L., Magnus, K., & Fagen, D. (1999). Caregiving and developmental factors differentiating young at-risk urban children showing resilient versus stress-affected outcomes: A replication and extension. *Child Development, 70,* 645–659.

Wyman, P., Cowen, E., Work, W. & Kerley, J. (1993). The role of children's future expectations in self-system functioning and adjustment to life-stress. *Development and Psychopathology, 5,* 649–661.

Wyman, P., Cowen, E., Work, W., & Parker, G. (1991). Developmental and family milieu interview correlates of resilience in urban children who have experienced major life-stress. *American Journal of Community Psychology, 19,* 405–426.

Wyman, P., Cowen, E., Work, W., Raoof, A., Gribble, P., Parker, G., & Wannon, M. (1992). Interviews with children who experienced a major life stress: Family and child attributes that predict resilient outcomes. *Journal of the American Academy of Child and Adolescent Psychiatry, 31,* 904–910.

Zigler, E. & Hall, N. (1989). Physical child abuse in America: Past, present, and future. In D. Cichetti & V. Carlson (Eds.), *Child maltreatment: Theory and research on the causes and consequences of child abuse and neglect* (pp. 38–75). New York: Cambridge University Press.

Zimmerman, B. (1995). Self-efficacy and educational development. In A. Bandura (Ed.), *Self-efficacy in changing societies* (pp. 202–231). Cambridge, UK: Cambridge University Press.

Zimmerman, J. (1996). *The way of council.* Las Vegas, NV: Bramble Books.

Free Reports Available from WestEd

Ensuring That No Child Is Left Behind
How Are Student Health Risks & Resilience Related to the Academic Progress of Schools?

Public schools are under enormous pressure to demonstrate academic gains on "high-stakes" standardized achievement tests. However, too many students come to school with developmental and health-related problems that make successful learning difficult, if not impossible. Schools seeking to improve student academic performance cannot ignore the role that health, school safety, caring relationships in the school, low rates of alcohol and other drug use, nutrition, and exercise play in their overall efforts. Based on data from the California Healthy Kids Survey administered by WestEd throughout the state, this report underscores the importance to academic achievement of key risk and youth development factors. According to this report, policies and practices that focus exclusively on raising test scores, while ignoring the comprehensive health needs of students, are likely to leave many children behind. A corresponding PowerPoint presentation is available that includes talking points and background information to enable anyone to make a presentation on the study results. To download your free PDF report, visit www.WestEd.org/cs/we/view/rs/740.

Thomas L. Hanson, Gregory Austin, & June Lee-Bayha

Order #: HD-04-02
Free PDF download available at www.WestEd.org/products
(Hardcopies available for purchase)

Bridging Cultures in Our Schools
New Approaches That Work
(Knowledge Brief)

"Teachers who serve each day as cultural mediators know the challenge goes beyond language. Even as they try to help immigrant students navigate a new system of education, their own teaching methods and most routine classroom expectations can come into perplexing conflict with children's cultural ways of knowing and behaving." – from the text

This Knowledge Brief provides a framework for understanding how teachers' culturally driven – and often unconsciously held – values influence classroom practice and expectations, and, when in conflict with the values of immigrant and other parents from more collectivistic societies, can interfere with parent-teacher communication. The brief looks at some specific sources of cross-culture conflicts and illustrates some strategies for resolving them. To download your free PDF report, visit www.WestEd.org/cs/we/view/rs/81.

Bridging Cultures Between Home and School Institute professional development is also available. Please contact Noelle Caskey at 415.615.3178 or ncaskey@WestEd.org.

Elise Trumbull, Carrie Rothstein-Fisch, & Patricia M. Greenfield

Order #: LCD-99-01
Free PDF download available at www.WestEd.org/products
(Hardcopies available for purchase)

To find information on our research and services, or to sign up for WestEd's monthly E-Bulletin newsletter and other free reports, visit www.WestEd.org.

Also available from WestEd

SERVICES

WestEd's resiliency workshops help teachers, counselors, health coordinators, after-school program staff, and school and district leaders understand and apply effective youth development approaches. The result? Programs that create more supportive and asset-rich environments that connect youth to their school communities, engage them in learning, promote their resilience, and reduce their involvement in substance use, violence, and other risk behaviors. Participants receive a manual containing supportive materials, a list of useful resources, a CD-ROM of workshops slides, and *Resiliency: What We Have Learned*. Four workshops are available:

Promoting Resilience and Youth Development in School Communities

"They should have this training at every school in America and make it a college requirement for all teachers...."

– Workshop Participant

From Risk to Resilience: Principles and Strategies of Youth Development

>> Research base for resilience and youth development

>> Prevention, youth education, and human services

>> Strategies to promote development assets critical to learning

>> Sources of support to sustain resilience practices

Listening to Youth: Using Youth Assets Data for School Community Improvement

>> Interpreting and using local Resilience and Youth Development Module data

>> Student focus groups for school community improvement

>> Creating research-based action plan based on student/staff recommendations

Using Youth Development for Comprehensive Safe Schools Planning

>> Linking caring school communities to safe schools

>> Creating caring communities with youth development principles

>> Meeting federal/state safe schools requirements using youth development approaches

"You Matter!": Promoting Resilience and Youth Development in After-School Programs

>> Principles of youth development

>> Major messages of resilience research

>> Power of caring relationships and positive expectations

>> Creating opportunities for participation and contribution

>> Developing strengths-based approaches in after school settings

Workshops are led by Bo De Long-Cotty and WestEd staff, all leading experts in youth development and resiliency. For information about the workshops or customized training, contact Bo De Long-Cotty at 510.302.4218 or bdelong@WestEd.org.